WHAT AN
IN THE TWE

Continuum Icons

Great books never go out of style, but they can go out of print. The Icons series is an attractively packaged collection of the greatest works of well-known authors. Enjoy them for the first time, or take some time to reacquaint yourself with these wonderful writers.

Books in the series include:

What Anglicans Believe

in

the Twenty-first Century

DAVID L. EDWARDS

continuum
LONDON • NEW YORK

Continuum

The Tower Building
11 York Road
London SE1 7NX

15 East 26th Street
New York
NY 10010

First published 2000, updated 2002
This edition published 2004

British Library Cataloguing-in-Publication Data
A catalogue record for this book is available from the British Library.

ISBN 08264–7689-9

Designed and typeset by Kenneth Burnley, Wirral, Cheshire.
Printed and bound in Great Britain by Cromwell Press Ltd,
Trowbridge, Wilts.

Contents

Preface

THIS BOOK BEGAN when I was asked to write an honest yet concise account of the Anglican way of being a Christian. It was to be personal and conversational, not official and formal, but the plan was to present agreements between Anglicans – or between most of them – rather than the views of a minority. My first reaction was that the job would not be easy and I advised the enterprising publisher to try other writers. It was only when they, too, had refused that I had a go.

I meant what I said in the Preface to the first edition in 1974: 'If I can help a single person to see what one Anglican (myself) believes about the things that matter, the book will be worthwhile.' So I am very thankful that tens of thousands of copies have been sold of the editions printed in Britain and the USA. The text was revised in 1999, and now I have been asked to explain why I hope that it will be found useful by private readers or discussion groups for some time to come.

I have learned that I can give the impression that I underestimate the problems involved nowadays in 'believing'. That may be inevitable if one tries to be both short and sharp, but actually I don't pretend that faith is easy. It is almost fifty years since I became a clergyman and in that time almost all the Churches in Britain and the rest of Europe have declined quite drastically in their active membership – and if the drop continues at its present rate, they will be extinguished. I know from experience that smaller Churches can flourish in a sense: their remaining members can love them, get a lot out of their membership, and be strong in their commitment. But when the statistics are grim, if there is to be a revival of wider support during the new century, it is obviously necessary to be something, and do something, and say something new. Even in parts of the world where the Churches flourish in ways which are reflected in encouraging statistics – in the USA, for example, or in southern Africa – life is changing fast. Anyway, in every place and time Churches depend on volunteers who eventually die, so that the message must be restated again and again in order to reach new generations. Churches are always in danger of dying.

In the part of the world which I know best, there are factors in the development of society which account for the decline of the Churches along with other large voluntary organizations. People are less interested in joining political parties, for example. But the biggest problem is, I think, the widespread feeling that it is unreasonable – or, at least, right out of fashion – to believe strongly in God. For many people 'God' has become three letters joined to make a swear-word. G, o and d can be used to add a little extra drama to an explosion of anger ('For God's sake!') or surprise ('Good God!') or relief ('Thank God!') or ignorance ('God knows!'), and when people say 'My God!' they don't intend to suggest a serious relationship. Most people see no point in joining a community which worships God regularly in a church, because there seem to be many more useful or relaxing things to do on a Sunday.

People may be aware that faith in God added sunshine to many lives in the past, but now God – or, at any rate, the God of the Churches – seems to be eclipsed. At first the experience may be very pleasant, for other lights go on in the evening. But the darkness which may be called the 'death of God' may in the end mean that for most people life has no ultimate purpose or meaning, that there is no great contrast between right and wrong, and that nothing is sacred. Already there are signs that this attitude is developing in the midst of all the attractions and benefits of a modern society.

In my own struggles I tell myself, and in this book I try to persuade or remind you, that nowadays anyone who really cares about the question of 'God' has to make a decision – and has to repeat it many times. Following public opinion cannot be enough if I really am to believe – or not believe. My answer to this question about God cannot be completely certain, for 'faith' means trust: it cannot mean knowledge which can be proved to be accurate. Nor can my decision be completely final, for it will have to be renewed or changed at every stage in life's journey. But it does not follow that faith is always weaker than knowledge and inferior to it. The most important things in our lives are things in which we believe – for example, that we are totally and permanently loved (about which no one who is not extremely conceited can be absolutely sure). We can give good reasons for having put our trust in someone or something, but we should never pretend that our decision is risk-free.

Nor does it follow that because it is often difficult to believe, it is more sensible to get on with life without bothering about such questions which can't be answered very simply. What we do depends on what we are – and what we are depends on what we believe. People sometimes say that 'being a real Christian' means living according to the Sermon on the Mount. But anyone who studies that teaching by Jesus in St Matthew's gospel (chapters 5, 6 and 7) will see that it is sensible only if God is what Jesus says he is. So what should we believe?

It is a tragedy that the Churches seem to most people too dogmatic with out-of-date dogmas. But they need not live in the past, for although the reality of God cannot be proved by science or by logic, many things in modern knowledge and life can support a decision to believe that God is more real than any other kind of reality. In these pages I shall point out that modern science has revealed the staggering immensity of the universe, in which the evolution of life on this planet is truly miraculous. Modern communications have brought into our homes and minds news which can very often be interpreted as a battle against evil by Good – and why not by God? Modern ideas about parenthood can help us to understand why God the Father or Mother is not a dictator. And modern awareness of the many threats to life on this planet can help us to see our world as a home which is fragile, given into our hands by our Creator, so that for the best of reasons it is vital that we should change our behaviour, and seek help to change. So it is possible to be a believer in a modern way.

Some tough questions to the Churches cannot be escaped, however. Why does God so often seem so old and so small? Why don't they have a great annual festival, as big as Christmas or Easter, celebrating the creation revealed to us by modern science and now in great danger? Why don't they talk less about themselves and their traditions – and more about the great hope that the 'kingdom' or government of God will be accepted on earth, to our great benefit? Why do they often preach that God is already in detailed control of everything that happens, when science, history and the tragedies in the news and in our own lives contradict that claim? Why aren't their leaders more outspoken in protests against the evils which often seem to have all the power? Why aren't their members more active in campaigns? And why aren't they happier?

I know that these questions are crude and unfair as I have expressed them. But I also know that they are often asked (I ask them myself) and that the Churches will have no great future unless they are answered, perhaps by some of the people who now ask them as critics.

The Churches do not only speak about and worship the Creator of all that exists. Their message is also about Jesus Christ – and again, Britain and the rest of Europe are now finding it hard to believe what the Churches are heard to be saying. The words 'Jesus Christ!' now provide another expression to be used when needing to swear. More gently, children are encouraged to act the story about his birth in nativity plays in primary schools, because it is such a lovely story; for adults Christmas is a festival of shopping, eating, drinking and sentimentality about our own family; his crucifixion adds a cross to a bun; at Easter he can sometimes be seen in public amid the daffodils and rabbits. It seems that many people can't forget Christ – or take him seriously.

In contrast, my chapters about him present him not only as the supreme teacher of the astonishing claim that the Creator of the universe is 'Love', but also as the unique embodiment of God's love in one human life. He proclaimed that love by living, working and dying as he did, and by the victory which followed his death. He gave all to his mission and that is why people have given their hearts to him. Much can be known about him as a figure in history but, as countless Christians have experienced, he can also be known as the living Christ of the centuries as they come and go. Like so many others, I have discovered that this living Christ challenges us to follow him now, as powerfully as when he challenged his first followers in Galilee. We don't completely understand or obey but he grips and commands us, and even if we stumble as we try to follow we learn all the time about him and therefore about God.

So who is Christ for us today? Clearly, new words are needed which will convey the life-changing excitement of meeting Christ, for real and for now. This book includes some words which now mean a lot to me, and I think to many others, but in the twenty-first Christian century new discoveries and new ways of speaking must and will come. So I hope that the main impact of these chapters will be to emphasize that being a Christian seriously must mean a commitment to Christ and his ongoing cause. Ours is a time when it is not easy to make that commitment, but Christ never said that following him would be a joy-ride.

On the contrary, the modern age is a time when many Christians have needed guts. They have often had to endure persecution, or being treated as second-class citizens, or being viewed with some pity as members of a minority thought to be trapped in nonsense. In countries tightly controlled by Nazi, Fascist, Communist or simply tyrannical and corrupt regimes, Christians loyal to Christ have needed courage to accept the possibility of martyrdom, or at least acute unpopularity. Around the world Christians have found themselves being tested, much as they were in Christianity's early years under the might of the Roman Empire. Christians have also been tested by being a minority living among neighbours who take a great pride in their own religious heritage. Of course, truth, goodness and holiness are found in many places outside the Churches – but the heart-searching question is: how is that fact to be acknowledged gladly while keeping oneself loyal to Christ? And decisions which are often not easy are necessary, day by day, when Christians live in a country which was nominally 'Christian' in the past but which now pays little attention to the question about God or to the challenge of Christ.

You can check your own response to one or other of these uncomfortable situations. If a government determined to stamp out Christianity came to power and you were arrested on suspicion of being a Christian, would this be enough evidence for the police to be able to secure your condemnation and punishment?

You will certainly not be able to be the kind of Christian that Christ wants (according to the New Testament) if you rely on your own strength or cleverness – and how well I know that! Nowadays we often hear about the human need for 'spirituality' amid materialism, because things which aren't physical (music is an example) deserve attention as parts of being fully human and money isn't everything. We need food for our minds and souls. But to be Christian, spirituality is more than the cultivation of the spiritual side of my own personality. It is being open, in company with many others, to the 'Spirit' or energy of the God who is within me but far, far greater than me. And so this book offers an essential chapter about God reaching us and remaking us, as 'Holy Spirit'.

I don't mean anything spooky and I am glad that this electrifying energy is no longer usually called by the old term in English, 'Holy Ghost'. Nor do I insist that the gift of the Spirit must be sensational. It may be accompanied by dramatic behaviour such as 'speaking in tongues' (in ecstasy): we are told that the first Christians were so excited that onlookers thought they were drunk. Certainly it produces a new flow of love for God, for his creation and for other people, and an upsurge of joy and confidence, and these changes may come in a rush – but when the excitement is over love, joy and hope have to continue coming every day. That makes most Christian experience of the Holy Spirit more like welcoming another shower of much needed rain and less like being caught in a thunderstorm. Nor do I pretend that the Holy Spirit only works in the Churches, although many Christians are clearly among those who are inspired to be, and do, better than what is natural. Nor do I claim that the Spirit is confined to the religions of the world. This energy comes from God, who is unlimited in his purpose to fill everyone with this blessing.

The Christian doctrine of the Holy Trinity should therefore never be treated as a piece of guesswork or as a mythological picture of three gods. It is because of what they have experienced for themselves that Christians have felt driven to say that the one true God has three ways of being God, all within human experience up to a point. God is the Creator of all that exists. God's loving purpose has been made known in the life of Jesus Christ, to reach, save and change us. And God's power to make us spiritually strong has been poured out in the gift of the Holy Spirit. Much remains a mystery but to worship the 'three-in-one' God is not to play a game: it is to be grateful for being rescued.

The rest of this little book presents my own convictions about what Anglicans ought to believe and be, as a result of real faith in the real God. I have delayed being 'denominational' (stressing any one of the many Churches) because I am passionately convinced that divisions between Christians ought to be reduced, not emphasized.

I don't pretend that all Anglicans agree about everything. Anglicanism is not an 'ism' in the sense of being an exactly defined and decreed system to control our thoughts and behaviour. Not only do Anglicans have different national, social and personal backgrounds influencing their religious life: some are by temperament more conservative than others, and within the ranks of those who are, on the whole, more conservative, some are more Catholic and others more Evangelical in their loyalty. But Anglicanism is not a do-it-yourself religion, and what unites Anglicans who think seriously about current problems is an acceptance of no fewer than three authorities.

The Bible's inspired message comes from God and can never be ignored or replaced by serious Christians. This is what Evangelicals stress. There is, however, a wise message to be learned from the believing and living of the whole Christian Church over the 2000 years of its history so far. This is what Catholics value. And like everyone else Christians ought to learn from modern knowledge and modern experience. This is what 'liberals' insist. Which authority is most important for a particular problem? It may not be easy to decide. The Bible witnesses to the coming of the 'Word of God' to Ancient Israel and then to those who first followed Christ – yet the Bible was written long ago and much has changed since then. The Church has brought the message of the Bible to the world, relating it to many new times and places – yet the officials of the divided Churches have been no more than human and have made many errors. Modern knowledge is growing all the time and modern life is changing (already some people talk about being post-modern), so that being modern does not always mean being right. Therefore Anglicans are challenged to think and decide and the right answers may not be immediately clear. I find nothing to be ashamed of in this situation.

Having these three authorities in mind, I have tried to state some answers which seem right to me, about questions important in modern life.

I have written about love as the greatest of all God's gifts, but I have not tried to define 'love' in ways which deny modern experience of it. Certainly I believe that the need to receive and give love is basic in human nature. Marriage is one of the most wonderful kinds of love, but I know that some marriages can break down precisely because they are relationships between free equals, and I am in no position to condemn a second marriage after a divorce. And I offer a few words about sex, although many people think that the only thing ever said by the Churches about sex is 'don't'. Marriage is most wonderful when it shares God's own power to create children, but I do not say that all sex outside marriage is equally wrong. I know that for most people love and joy can be overwhelming when 'boy meets girl', but I do not deny that some people, including Christians, are by nature homosexual and are convinced that it is right to express their sexuality physically; I cannot condemn them. I respect those Anglican teachers who are more cautious about these controversial topics but I do not agree with them, and neither do many other Anglicans.

We have a healthy instinct to be as happy as we can be, but Christianity is one of the sources of wisdom warning us against some dangerous or disastrous quests for happiness. We all need to shop and consume, but that should not degrade us into consumerism as the meaning of life: we are not born to shop. It is closer to the truth taught by life to say that the best way to find happiness is to find friendship – which is nearly always possible, since friends can be made if we are friendly and the most lonely of us can be friends with God.

Jesus warns us in particular against nursing hatred in our hearts, so I have written (I hope realistically) about forgiveness. Since God is the supreme Forgiver, 'heaven' is enjoying for ever his merciful love and 'hell' is refusing to be forgiven and cleansed so that we may share his glory. According to Jesus himself, the faith that is needed is the desire to 'see' God and be with him – our greatest joy.

In the light which reaches us from the story of Christ, Christianity cannot be the enemy of freedom despite the intolerance which has often been an evil in the history of the Churches. The Christian Church is made up of a great variety of people who are free to be themselves, whatever some church leaders may have said. What unites them is that they have been freed (at least to some extent) from addictions and prejudices which make us slaves; when I depend on a drug or 'what people say', I am not free to be myself. To be converted as a Christian is to be liberated.

To pray as a Christian is chiefly to enjoy the company of the God who has liberated us and to listen to him, and so we need to pray, and to be taught by Christ and the Holy Spirit how to pray. To live as a Christian is to live as a member of the Christian Church, for Christ never intended that his followers should go it alone. Sometimes people say 'go into the Church' meaning 'be ordained', but Christians go into the Church when they are baptized and the Church asks that from that day to their deaths life should consist of learning what baptism implies. Sometimes people contrast 'Bible' and 'Church', and clearly the Bible can criticize the Church. But the Bible is the Church's book – or, rather, a library of short books which, when taken together, tell how God has made himself known, first to Ancient Israel and then through Christ to the Church in its first century.

It is only after discussing all these things (however briefly and inadequately) that I attempt to say what is distinctively Anglican about this version of Christianity. Here I shall say only a little. I am very glad and proud that I have been an Anglican since my baptism as a baby. In all my adult life I have depended on frequent sharing in the Holy Communion as celebrated by Anglicans. Becoming an Anglican priest was for me very far from being a mistake, for in my experience the clergy are the servants of the Christian people because they are the servants of Christ, and as such they have great rewards. I have found my own Church, the Church of England, to be a kind of family in which I have usually felt at home – for it is a very tolerant family, not without arguments but certainly with bonds of affection and celebrations of shared happiness. Yet I am sure that Anglicanism as it exists cannot be permanent, and should not be. In my last chapter I therefore say a little about what I believe is desirable as we turn to the future. I know that many others share these hopes.

Here I add only two points, for I wish that I had been more emphatic about them when I last revised the text. As I write, many people are being killed because of the hatred between the Israelis and the Palestinians in the land of the Bible, the 'Holy Land'; and two poor but proud nations, India and Pakistan, fire shells at each other in Kashmir and advertise their possession of nuclear weapons. And the destruction by terrorists of the World Trade Centre in New York showed that no nation can be completely secure. Conflicts between religions have been involved – or have been used – in all these tragedies. So friendly conversation and co-operation between all religious believers can be seen, more clearly than ever before, to be absolutely essential. No less vital is the need for the international community to wage war against the spread of modern weapons – and not only weapons of mass destruction, for 'ordinary' guns are disastrously spread all over Africa, for example. Terrorism and aggression must be resisted but we also have to resist taking all those weapons for granted. All this calls for urgent campaigning by the Churches – and not only by the American Churches, which have great influence in the world's only superpower, because even in Britain and the rest of Europe the Churches can be heard if they will speak up.

More cheerfully, I ought to have celebrated more fully the leadership of women in the Churches, since my Church is about to discuss having women bishops. What can be called the feminine strengths are needed in the Churches no less than in the nations. I am delighted that I have lived to see women being allowed to become Anglican priests and I hope that there will be more and more of them. All through the history of Christianity women have been more active, more sensible and more attractive than men in maintaining the life of prayer and in drawing others to Christ. I hope and pray that this contribution will grow, to make Christianity's next 2000 years rather more in keeping with the hope and prayer of Christ.

But I have not changed the text, for I am sure there are other gaps in it which you can spot. I want to remind myself, and you, that decisions which will shape the Christian Church of the future will be made not by an old man such as me but by new generations of believers who in response to new problems will trust with all their hearts and minds in God through Christ, in the power which is the gift of the Holy Spirit.

DAVID L. EDWARDS

CHAPTER ONE

We begin to believe

HAVE YOU MET GOD? The question is clearly very different from asking whether you happened to meet a friend in the street. If he is real, God must be greater than anyone or anything else – and greater than our thoughts about him. God is usually referred to as 'he', but of course that does not mean that 'he' is male. If he exists, his existence is not limited like the existence of people and things; he does not begin or end, he is the source of all existence. So if he is there, getting to know him must be our most important job between birth and death. And yet God is invisible. He does not speak as people speak; he does not act as people act; he does not live in your street or in anyone else's. It can be thought that he does not exist at all – that people's hopes or fears about him are all based on a simple mistake.

That is the mysterious God, mysteriously great, mysteriously different, mysteriously fascinating, but often mysteriously difficult to get to know. So how can we meet God and find out whether he is the great reality or the great illusion?

Usually we hear about him from quite an early age. Religion may mean a lot in the place we come from, or the contact between our family or school and a religious tradition may not be very active; but in either case the idea of God comes into our lives along with other ideas which are easier to grasp. While we are very young we are in no position to argue, but we reach a time when we ask questions, enjoying in particular the questions which adults themselves find very hard to answer. More painfully, we ask ourselves who we really are: 'I'm me' but actually what is my personality, my style, and where do I genuinely belong? And who or what is my God? We may try to get rid of such questions by deciding to think and do what the group around us thinks and does, but the questions will not go away. They are a part of being human.

This book is written for people who think for themselves and who are willing to think about God. Its writer has tried to be totally honest. If God has given us brains to use, and if his reality is the biggest truth there is, he cannot possibly object to our asking what is the truth about him. And if he has surrounded himself with mystery, he cannot be at all surprised or angry if we find it difficult to reach the truth, sometimes disagreeing with each other, sometimes abandoning what we ourselves believed at an earlier stage. If he is real yet hidden from us, it must be that he values, more highly than we expected, our freedom to think for ourselves and to meet him for ourselves.

This book will say that thinking about God involves believing. That does not imply that religious believers have a good excuse to believe in nonsense. If I believe that the moon is made of cheese I am simply wrong; someone may return from space with a piece of rock from the moon and that is the end of my theory, even if I claim that I held the theory because I am religious. Like everyone else, religious believers ought to accept every fact that can be proved scientifically, and ought to reject every theory that can be known to be nonsense.

What this book will argue is that believing in God is like believing in a friend. When we get to know someone, it is bit by bit, step by step. Gradually we form our own impressions about that person's character. We begin to feel that we can guess how she will behave in a new situation, and we begin to be confident that she will want to behave in a way that is best for us. But all the time it will be possible for an onlooker to say in gossip: 'I can't see what he sees in her.' And all the time it will be possible that the trust will turn out to have been a mistake, for this kind of believing, trusting that a friend is reliable, can never be knowledge which can be demonstrated to be true. In real life, this trust in a personal relationship is too big and too important to be tested by research in a laboratory. And in much the same say, believing in God is a trust which cannot be proved to be either sensible or unwise. No one can produce the final, knock-down proof that God is real and good, and therefore reliable – or that he isn't.

But some evidence is available that God is what Christians claim he is. In this book something will be said about the Bible. This is not because the Bible is a camera which has recorded everything accurately. Nor is it a single book which was dictated by God to a secretary. The Bible is a collection of books written by different people at different times in different styles about different subjects, and always using human words. But it is also a collection of witnesses to the activity of God and to his character. It is a little library with a unique authority, for Christians believe that these people were witnesses to the most important activity of God in history, reaching its climax in the life, teaching, death and victory of Jesus. So the Bible can speak to us.

Something will also be said about the Christian Church, and in particular about the Anglican tradition within the wider Church. That is not because the Church is a perfect institution. It is a collection of people, with all the flaws to be expected when human nature is at work. The history of the Church includes many mistakes and many tragedies. But the Church is itself a witness to the activity of God, specially to what God did – and goes on doing – through the life of Jesus and through the spiritual power which can overcome our weakness and our evil.

The Anglican tradition is only one part of Christianity. The word 'Anglican' comes from the Latin for 'English' and a major role in Anglican history has been played by the Church of England. But today the Anglican Communion is a fellowship which is world-wide, although in most places its numbers are small in comparison with other churches or other religions. Every year it becomes less distinctively English, and every year it sees more clearly how much it has to learn from fellow Christians who are not Anglicans – and how much it has to give. It can share with others the good results of an experiment which was made in England. From the sixteenth century onwards the Church of England has been Protestant or Reformed, accepting reforms made after protests against errors and evils which had developed in the Church during the Middle Ages. More positively, the Church of England is evangelical, meaning that it puts its emphasis on the message of the Bible, on our need to accept that message definitely and to spread it, on the simplicity and directness of personal prayer, and on the challenge to live up to the ideal of Christian morality in daily life.

But Anglicans have always valued and kept many things from the catholic form of Christianity. That has meant keeping and using the sacraments, specially the Eucharist or Holy Communion. The catholic emphasis is on order and dignity in public worship, on a feeling of fellowship with all the saints of all the ages, and on a beauty in churches which ought to encourage beauty in lives. And the mission of the local church is strengthened when churches are grouped together in a diocese led by a bishop.

These things are the heritage for which Anglicans are grateful. They help us to believe in God – and to meet him. Other Christians are helped by some, many or all of the same things, and they can help Anglicans to appreciate them more deeply. But it seems to be the special role of the Anglican tradition to hold all these things together. Individuals are free to value most the things which help them most, so that there are 'evangelical' Anglicans and 'catholic' Anglicans. But Anglicans are frequently reminded – whether by controversies or by friendships – that there are others who find other bits of the tradition valuable. It is like members of a team, or an orchestra, having their own things to do but not being able to do much without each other.

Anglicans are free to develop their own ways of understanding. They are encouraged to take very seriously both the Bible and the history of the Church, and to be guided by those authorities – but the response to those authorities must be their own, for they must think and act according to their consciences. It is like having a map in a strange town but needing to use one's own feet and courage. Many people treasure the traditional expressions of Christian beliefs, which satisfied many saints for many centuries. Others, specially those called 'liberals', want to work out new ways of absorbing and communicating these beliefs in a world which is very different from the past. Whether we are 'liberals' or not, always the attempt must be made to find and speak the truth. Always there must be fellowship with Christians who see things differently. But always in the end each person must speak the truth as he or she has found it.

That is why this presentation of 'what Anglicans believe' is a statement by one Anglican, who can make mistakes, who must be open to correction, but who hopes never to be disobedient to the truth. And this short book will try to develop themes which have been mentioned in this even shorter introduction.

CHAPTER TWO

We believe in God

It isn't simple . . .

Is it reasonable to believe in God? Nowadays many people are far from sure that it is, although not many people say that they are convinced atheists. ('Atheism' means that you are sure there is no God. 'Agnosticism' means that you can't decide whether there is or isn't. Many people are agnostics.)

We must face the fact that belief in God can easily turn into mere superstition or sentimentality, which is against all reason. People can have gods whose job is to give them assistance in their private ambitions – or to help their tribe or nation to win a war or to grow a good harvest. Or people can have a god who is like a painted piece of wood or like an old man with a beard in the sky.

It is also a fact that people can say that evil attitudes are commanded by the god they worship. They can say that their god wishes them to be arrogant, intolerant and cruel – or that their god wishes them to contradict what is known scientifically. People calling themselves Christians have tried to justify their evil attitudes in these ways.

It is, however, possible to seek the real God. Indeed, it is not only possible – nowadays it is necessary if you are to believe in God.

In the old days almost everyone had to accept the beliefs which were taken for granted in the society around them, and one of the beliefs it was dangerous to question was belief in God (or gods). But in our society there is religious freedom, which from every point of view is a great gain. It frees those who don't believe from the need to pretend; and it brings many benefits to sincerely religious people. For it means that you have to make your own search to find God – just as you have to make your own search to find a wife or a husband. In that adventure, you grow spiritually. You have to make up your own mind – and so your mind is made your own.

No words, however pure or sacred, will fully describe God. Indian spiritual teachers say something about God to which we ought to listen. They say: 'Not that! Not that!' In the Middle Ages a council of the Catholic Church agreed that when God is compared with anyone or anything, there is more unlikeness. The same emphasis on the mystery of God is found in the Bible. For God can never be pinned down like a dead butterfly, reduced to a formula or reproduced in a photograph. No talk about God can be completely accurate, because all such talk must use words which were invented to describe the world or the people in it – not God. Like shots which always miss their target, human words will always fall short of the glory of God. But the words can show in what direction the glory lies; however imperfectly, they can point to the reality. For example, when we say that God is 'personal' we must admit that he cannot be a person as we are people. He is not one person among many people. He must be much more. But the word 'personal' points to the reality that, if he is real, God cannot be less than personal – for he cannot be less than us. It also points to the experience that if we pray God can make himself known to us in a relationship which feels person-to-person.

God has been called 'the most real thing there is'. The trouble is that we often keep the idea of God in a separate compartment of our mind – and we often keep all the things that are immediately important to us (health, money, sex, music, our job, our family, today's news, a personal tragedy) in other compartments which we think of as more realistic. But if God is real, then he is more real than the greatest thing or the best thing or the worst thing in the rest of our experience. Indeed, he is not one thing among many things. If God exists at all, God is utterly unique: God is God and everything depends on God.

But even if you make up your mind that God is real, you will never 'know' this in the way that you can know the truth of a formula in chemistry or a fact in the newspaper. Until you die, you will always need faith and your faith will always be attacked by doubts, since if you 'believe', you always have to admit that you may be wrong, even if you only admit it to yourself. If you believe, it is like swimming in water – where you could drown. This may alarm you. But just as there can be no sure proof of God, so also there can be no sure disproof. You simply have to decide for yourself – and that goes for atheists too.

. . . but it isn't wrong

Without being unreasonable you can have enough confidence to decide that for all practical purposes you are prepared to bet your life that God is there. Of course we run the risk of being wrong. But just as a scientist makes an experiment in order to test a theory, so you can put belief in God to the test – by living in the light of it. Then you will find yourself increasingly assured about God's reality.

Sometimes this kind of assurance can come to us suddenly, like a flash. Some people have dramatic experiences which persuade them that God is real. Even in those cases, however, the search for the real God has probably been going on for a long time. Normally it takes a long time to reach the strong relationship with God that produces confidence.

There is an answer to the people who promise you that you can have the vision by swallowing a drug. What people see when under the influence of a drug is an illusion produced by chemistry, and it quickly fades – leaving behind problems. And there is an answer to the people who tell you that you can't find God without reading strange books or going to distant countries. God is closer to you than your feet or your hands or your breath.

Experience has convinced many millions of people that the best way to God is to be quiet before this mystery – to meditate, which means thinking calmly, slowly, deeply. Think about God much more than about yourself, want God more than you want anything for yourself, but try to make sure that there is love in your heart and peace in your mind, so that you are not distracted by any foolishness. Say to God: 'If you are real, give me the eyes to glimpse your reality.' Ask God to give you that glimpse, even if it means showing you that you will have to change your own ways of thinking and behaving.

We have to concentrate, again and again. It is a discipline, like learning a language or learning to drive a car. But many of the finest characters and greatest minds in history have made the same search before us. And people who seriously seek the real God find that no one goes unrewarded. So we have to say to ourselves: 'This search is the most important task I shall ever attempt. This adventure is going to take all I have, but my aim is to find the greatest treasure that could possibly exist.'

When we seek the meaning in life, we are seeking God. For in the end, when all things which for the moment keep us excited or busy have died down, there can't be much meaning if there is no God! And when we seek God, we express a hunger. Every other hunger corresponds with some food which can satisfy it. Despite our doubts and hesitations about belief in God, the alternative is grim – an ultimately meaningless life, a largely frustrated hunger of the spirit for meaning. Doesn't that imply that deep down you are already inclining towards the decision to believe in God? A French mathematician, Blaise Pascal, wrote more than three hundred years ago that he seemed to hear God saying to him: 'Comfort yourself, you would not seek me if you had not found me.' A great saint, Augustine of Hippo, looked back over his long search for God with this prayer: 'You have made us for yourself, and our heart is unquiet until it rests in you.' And many Christians, as they have looked back, have thought that the deepest reality was that God had been searching for them, that their faith was God's gift to them.

Remind yourself of the marvellous and often alarming features which have persuaded many to worship the mighty God – a glorious sunset over a city, countless stars in the night sky, the ocean in a storm, mountains, lions, the music of a symphony. (What is missing from that list?) Meditate also on the small things: an obscure animal so perfectly adapted to life, a rose, bird-song, light on water, dew on grass, a human baby, a girl's face, an athlete's health. (What is missing?) These things may be clues to aid your own search for the answer to the riddle of existence.

We must be honest. There are many things about our lives, about all human life, about the world around us, and about the universe, that make it hard to believe in God. There is darkness around us. But also light! For many things are indeed hard to explain if there is no God and therefore no good purpose running through it all. Atheism has its problems . . .

Why does anything exist, rather than nothing?

If the universe is nothing more than an accident, how has it happened that it contains so much order and so much beauty? It has been said that it works like a machine, yet sleeps like a picture. And it is amazing that what followed the initial 'Big Bang' developed in such a way that this planet was formed about ten thousand million years later – and became a home for life.

At point after point the development of the universe could have made it impossible for us to be here. But here we are, with hearts open to the wonder of it all, with minds stretched in order to be able to understand a bit of our backgrond. Why are we here?

The machinery of evolution can be understood. There are many mutations (genetic changes), and out of these the fittest – those best adapted to the struggle for food – survive. So chance comes into it. But does the whole process consist of nothing more than chances which are selected by the iron necessities of life? Is the universe merely a lottery or a bingo hall? If so, how has it happened that there has been such amazing progress? How has sheer chance produced Shakespeare and Beethoven, Einstein and Rembrandt?

If we can understand nothing about any purpose in the universe, how has it happened that we can understand so much else? Looking up a telescope or down a microscope, the scientist increasingly understands what he sees. The poet, the artist or the musician is able to celebrate the order and the beauty. And countless people have a basic feeling that our lives do make sense because we are meant to serve a purpose greater than ourselves. It has often been said that, despite all its faults, humanity believes in the supreme importance of beauty, truth and goodness. Everyone has at least glimmerings of those beliefs. Many people regard them as more important than comfort, ease or ambition. People often struggle to create beauty, to reach the truth, to do what seems right – whatever the cost. People are happy to spend their lives in these tasks, and they are prepared to die for the sake of these causes. A human being seems to be an animal that does not merely want to survive: look in the mirror and you will see the strangest animal in the world. How has it happened that such a 'freak' has been born?

These are questions which atheists find hard to answer – as believers in God find it hard to answer the problem of the existence of evil. In the end we have to decide whether the good seems to us more significant than the evil. We have to make up our own mind whether we are to be guided by the light we see, or by the darkness. People can meet this challenge in different ways which are equally honest. But there is no need to agree with the atheists that every thought about God has been proved to be a complete illusion. On the contrary, much of the evidence points to God – the God who is there beyond the ideas and pictures.

These thoughts can help you to believe, as a map made by previous travellers can guide you on a long journey into a strange country. But no argument can force you to believe. Only your own experience, as you understand it, can give you a living faith in the real God. So this question about God comes addressed to you personally.

CHAPTER THREE

The Father

The ultimate maker

God is called the Creator. That does not mean having a theory about how the universe began or how life began. Scientists are the only people competent to answer such questions – and although science made very exciting progress in the nineteenth and twentieth centuries, even scientists do not yet have all the answers. Believing in God the Creator means giving an answer to some very different questions: *why* the universe began, *why* life emerged, *why* the universe continues to exist with life on this planet (at least).

The astonishing truth seems to be that God wishes the universe and life into existence out of love – and God has not changed his mind. God loves all creatures great and small, and ultimately his love is what gives them their life. Believing in God the Creator means being grateful for this gift which is wonderful beyond anything which words can describe. The universe minus God would equal nothing. But as things are, the universe is a marvel from beginning to end, the birth of a baby is a miracle, and we are sensible to be filled with wonder and awe.

If that seems to be true, a question arises which many people think cannot be answered at all. It does not seem that the Creator has programmed the universe so that it functions like a computer which works perfectly and delivers exactly what was planned. On the contrary, as with the workings of computer viruses, much seems to go wrong. Many events are beyond our understanding: for example we cannot understand why the Creator has made a universe which is so large that the statistics about it include so many noughts that our minds become a blank. And many events seem to be contrary to what little we understand about the Creator's purpose: our planet is a scene of much suffering. If God is the source of all that exists, why has he created a universe so full of mysteries and tragedies?

Many people have believed in more than one god. One part of life seems so different from another that it is tempting to say that each part has its own ruler. So one god sends sunshine, and another god sends rain; one god sends happiness, and another god sends disasters; one god sends life, and another god sends death; one god looks after one country, and another god looks after its neighbour; one god is real on Sunday, and another on Monday. But always progress in religion comes from people saying that, however difficult it is to be sure of this unity, the universe is one, life is one, life's meaning is one, God the Creator and Ruler is one. Why, then, does the one Creator and Ruler allow so much evil to exist? For the Christian the problem is acute because what is at stake is the question whether God is both real and good.

We are not using the word 'God' and meaning by it only nature. God is bigger than nature. God is in everything, but he is more. All space is (so to speak) his body, but he is also beyond space, 'infinite'. And all time is (so to speak) his life, but he is also beyond time, 'eternal'. What someone makes (for example, a chair or a film) is that maker's achievement, but the maker remains different from what is made. So what God creates does not exhaust his endless life. He is the ultimate maker – but that is not all there is to him. And he is not only bigger than nature: he is also better. He is 'holy' – uniquely, divinely good. And so the question is: why does this good God allow so much evil to exist?

Fortunately for us, Jesus put his own teaching about God in a simple way. There are two key ideas in it.

The first is that God is taking action which will show the power of his love. He will show that he is Creator, and Ruler, and good. In other words, the 'kingdom' (which means 'rule') of God is coming. Jesus taught that nothing matters more than being alert and ready to respond to this action by God. This is an extremely practical matter. As we live each day, our biggest job is to serve the kingdom of God. As we watch TV or read the newspaper or meet neighbours or go to work, we can see the ways in which God's purpose is being obeyed or resisted in the world today. This gives a wealth of meaning to our life and to the world, since God is already at work in order to set up his government over the whole world; and he calls us, very urgently, to co-operate with him.

Jesus' favourite method of teaching was to tell a story (a parable). Almost always a parable has one big idea, and almost always that point is to make people more alert and ready as the kingdom of God comes. All the material in these stories was taken from the daily life familiar to Jesus and his first hearers. One way of understanding what was meant is to ask ourselves how the same point could be made in a story using material with which we are familiar 2,000 years later. In the world that we see out of the window or on the screen, God is busy.

The second main teaching of Jesus is that, even before his kingdom has fully come, God can be prayed to as 'Father'. The Lord's Prayer, which is a simple pattern for all Christian prayer, begins 'Father!' In his letters Paul twice quoted the actual word originally used by Jesus in the language he spoke, Aramaic; it is *Abba*, the equivalent is our 'Dad' or 'Daddy'. Does that seem childish? Actually Jesus was the opposite of childish. He used this word to teach a very mature understanding of God. This word expressed not only his attitude to God as a child but also his reliance on God as an adult – a reliance tested by much disappointment and suffering. Jesus was a poor man; a lonely, misunderstood man; a man who spent much of his time with the sick and the despised; a man who expected a terribly cruel death.

To call God 'Father' is only a way of speaking, and we can also think of God as 'Mother' or as 'Friend'. What matters is that this use of human figures *is* a way of speaking – to God. Instead of keeping silence at a distance, we speak up and come closer to God, although we know that God is greater than we can imagine. The Lord's Prayer reminds us of this when it immediately adds that the Father to whom we pray is beyond space and time – 'heavenly'. And the meaning is not at all sentimental. God's name or nature is 'holy'. To remember this is to worship. People may have an attitude close to worship towards a star in entertainment or sport – or towards a new car. All the fascination, delight and respect felt here are no more than clues to what a worshipper of God feels.

We can find here clues to the mystery of why God permits so much evil in his world. A good parent may be very loving and yet not want the children to lead a soft life because the strength which is developed by coping with tough problems cannot be obtained in any other way. And a good parent will often leave important decisions to their children to make up their own minds, preferring that they should choose the good freely. It is clear that God gives us a life full of problems and allows us much freedom, however dangerous this may be. And the explanation is this: he is 'Father'.

Treat the world as a home

If we regard the world as a battleground between good and evil, we do not see it as one big beach where we can snooze in the sun. But if we think of the world as God's creation, then the world is no longer a jumble we cannot make sense of. It is no longer hostile and frightening. It is not under the control of devils. Nor is it ruled completely by blind chance. However vast or dark it may seem, the place where we live is our home.

That means being happy in it – and honouring it. The other people in it belong to our family, whatever the colour of their skins or the sound of their talk. In their veins is the same red blood that runs in ours, and in their hearts are the same mixed feelings. And the whole earth deserves our respect, just as we respect the walls and the furniture of our home. The soil, water and air of this planet are precious. The earth's beauty, efficiency and (often) convenience to us are marvellous. But gratitude is not always the way we treat the world in practice. If this were our daily attitude, the environment which has been provided for us would not be so often damaged or wrecked by our carelessness, greed or cruelty. There would not be so much bitter conflict and misery in the news, and the future of human life on the earth would not be in doubt. We have failed, and we know it. So we feel about our lives as a whole as we feel about some disgraceful thing we have done: we feel guilty.

Many people nowadays feel dissatisfied with their lives, but they don't think they ought to feel guilty, because they don't feel responsible. They blame it on their parents, or their governments, or their glands. They say that they can't help it, for they are entirely the creatures of circumstances. To such people, the good news is the message that they are more than the stooges of fate and more than pathological cases. Whatever handicaps they may have inherited, however damaging their situation may be, they are, when all is said and done, responsible for what they do and become. Despite all their circumstances, their wills are to some extent free. They are not always forced to be the prisoners of their past: they are responsible for the future.

But once people see that they are able to be responsible, they may be overcome by feelings of guilt, so we may long to own up and clear the air – to express guilt and get rid of it. Jesus announced that such an opportunity exists. It is possible to go to God as to an understanding and affectionate parent. We can say 'sorry' to the Creator and the Ruler – and we can be heard by the Father. In the great traditional words, we can 'confess' our 'sin'. And whenever anyone turns to God in that way, God wipes away the past – whatever the past may have been. God does not do this grudgingly. God loves doing it, for he does it out of love. Jesus often said that his message was like an invitation to a banquet.

Instead of guilt, there is gratitude in the hearts of those who respond. Almost everyone enjoys life on the whole, and often feels thankful for it. Without God we have no one to thank – and no one to whom we can say 'sorry'. A person who worships God as Father or Mother will want to fill his prayers with thanksgiving for all the good things of life, which without exception are now valued as gifts coming from God. When we receive gifts, for example at Christmas, we feel that the fun is spoiled if the label gets lost, because then we 'don't know who it's from'. Half the pleasure of getting a gift is knowing whom to thank.

The life of a happy family provides one more clue to the meaning of Christianity, and it is the most important clue of all. Unless the family has been tragically broken up by bitterness, every son or daughter knows that nothing can change the basic attitude of parents. Whatever the son or the daughter does, Father carries on being a father and Mother remains a mother. And if you believe in God the Father, or Mother, you believe that you are loved – not only the 'good' bits of you, but you as you really are now. You belong. You are accepted. You have your place in the family, and nothing can take it away. This doesn't mean that you become lazily content with what you are. It does mean that you accept what you are – as the place to begin becoming what you think God wants you to be. You no longer hate or underestimate yourself. For if your Father who made you loves you, who are you to disagree?

CHAPTER FOUR

We believe in Jesus Christ

The living Christ

The word 'Christ' is not a surname like Williams or Smith. It comes from a Greek word translating the Hebrew word 'Messiah', which refers to the longed-for Liberator who would be sent by God to lead Israel into freedom and the world into a new glory. It is a word full of meaning historically – as is shown by (for example) Handel's masterpiece in music, *Messiah*, which is full of quotations from the Old Testament. So the phrase 'Jesus the Christ' immediately shows us that this first-century Jew, Yeshua of Nazareth, has been regarded as the King of the Jews. It also shows us that Jesus was a real figure in history – in Jewish history. But if his significance for us today is to be described in language which means a lot to us, it must be in words which have a modern meaning.

Jesus has had a greater influence than any other person in the whole course of history. Almost everyone would agree that it has been an influence for great good. Indeed, very many millions of people (not all of them Christians) would call him the best teacher who has ever lived. But Christians want to say more: that in the life of Jesus, God is embodied.

There was darkness surrounding the search for God – now a light has shone. When people cried to God, God often seemed silent – now a voice has spoken. When people were in distress, God often seemed distant – now he has come. When people asked questions, God often did not seem to be there at all – now he is here in person. When people complained about their suffering and death, God came to suffer and die. That is what Christians believe about Jesus, and it is worth taking trouble to work out the meaning of these beliefs in a way that is real for us.

We can begin with solid history, for it is certain that Jesus lived in Palestine about 2,000 years ago. It is also certain that he was executed by the Roman punishment of crucifixion, which shows that the Romans then occupying Palestine thought that he was guilty of being a rebel or of encouraging rebellion. No description of Jesus by the Romans survives, although the historians Tacitus and Suetonius mention him. The evidence that exists makes it certain, however, that Jesus was not a rebel in the ordinary sense of that word. This evidence consists almost entirely of some of the letters written by Paul within about thirty years of the death of Jesus – and four gospels which are not full biographies but which do contain much reliable information. Coming from five very different sources, this evidence enables us to reconstruct a kind of portrait of Jesus. And it shows us a man whose rebellion was religious, more than political.

His message was revolutionary because he announced that God's 'kingdom' was about to come – indeed, that it had already begun to come. But while the rest of the Jews waited for a Messiah who would be a national military leader, Jesus claimed that God was already acting decisively to show his rule and love – not by defeating the Jews' enemies in a war, but by answering doubters, healing the sick, overcoming the barriers of prejudice, and assuring sinners of forgiveness. In particular, Jesus claimed that God could now be known as Father.

This teaching was brilliantly expressed in short stories or powerful sayings. Much of it was remembered, and some of it was written down in four gospels (probably between 30 and 60 years after Jesus' crucifixion). But the evidence suggests that it was not the teaching that made the main impact. In fact, the gospels state that a great deal of the teaching was not understood at the time by even the closest followers of Jesus. What made the impact was that Jesus lived as he taught. He not only said that God was answering doubters – he commanded some people to leave everything and follow him. He not only said that God was healing the sick – he cured some people, even when it meant breaking the religious law that no work was to be done on the 'Sabbath' (Saturday). He not only said that God was forgiving sinners – he had friendly meals with some people who were notorious. He not only said that God was doing something new –

for some crushed people, he made a new start possible. His own life was new – and so was theirs.

And this life went on after his crucifixion – not only in the influence which heroes often have, and not only in the memory of his character, but much more personally and powerfully. He was tortured to death in public (a hateful memory for his friends to have), yet his followers claimed that they saw him, they felt his presence as surely as in the days when he had walked and talked with them along the roads of Galilee, as surely as on the evenings when, gathering his friends like a family, he had divided the loaf and poured out the wine. Their mysterious meetings with Jesus after his death were experiences which transformed their lives – giving them a new confidence, a new happiness and a new conviction that they were united with their Master and could never be separated from him. Their minds had been confused and their hearts broken; but now they were full of courage and faith, ready for hard lives and hard deaths. Something happened to change these men and women. That 'something' we call the 'resurrection' of Jesus.

Was the resurrection an experience in the mind? Clearly it was – but it was not dreamed up by these people. They responded to an event which happened and which convinced them. Was the resurrection of Jesus physical? The gospels in the Bible say that the tomb of Jesus was empty, and that his 'risen' body could be seen and touched. This is evidence which will be taken very seriously by modern people who have been impressed by Jesus himself – and by the moral and spiritual power of the first Christians. Although it makes a very strange story, it is illogical to limit the things that God can do – and very strange things happen in this world (especially in those events said to be communications with the dead which are investigated by 'psychical research'). The four gospels, however, describe the 'risen' body of Jesus as no ordinary body – it could go through doors, appear and disappear. And they do not provide us with an account which satisfies our curiosity about these very strange things. The details are different in the different gospels. So it seems that it is impossible to know exactly what happened. Whatever it was, it was neither psychological nor physical in the ordinary sense. But all Christians have good grounds for believing that something absolutely unique in its character and effects, something of the very greatest significance, did occur.

After it, the whole world was seen in a new light. The men and women who were prepared to follow Jesus could know in their hearts that he could never be defeated. That was their light. And the same light has come to Christians ever since. To live as people who believe in the resurrection of Jesus is to live triumphantly, with a happiness which can never be taken away.

And ever since the resurrection, Christians have known that Jesus' own good news about the kingdom and the Fatherhood of God is no longer enough. The Christian message certainly repeats what Jesus taught. But it is also now a message about Jesus himself. The followers of Jesus were soon nicknamed Christians or 'Christ-people' because they were always talking about Jesus Christ. To them, the supreme fact was that they had a personal relationship with the living Christ.

Who is he?

Two men who wrote gospels preserved in the New Testament, Luke and Matthew, were artists using words, probably often words already used and loved by other Christians. As they put these words together into stories, they were so inspired that their stories have touched the hearts and minds of people numerous beyond counting. These were stories not only about the resurrection of Jesus, but also about his birth – not only about the first Easter, but also about the first Christmas. They were not stories of the kind we now expect from serious newspapers or history books, giving us facts in a style which is detached from all feelings and neutral about all opinions. They were stories told vividly by people who were on fire with a faith – the faith that at the deepest level of its meaning knew that the birth of Jesus was the result of God's love for the world, the death of Jesus was the supreme embodiment of that love, and the resurrection of Jesus was the announcement by the Father of the victory of love. That was – and is – the glory glimpsed by humble people such as shepherds, and the light followed by wise people who make journeys of the mind and spirit in search of solutions to the greatest questions. That was – and is – the eyes-opening joy which can come to sad and frightened people when they see that Jesus will be with them, to the end of every road in the world.

The two greatest thinkers in that first Christian generation, Paul and John, put their eloquence into the task of stating what Jesus Christ meant in his own person as well as in his teaching. Inevitably they stated this mostly by describing Jesus as the climax of the Old Testament. In the course of a long debate among those early theologians whom we call the 'Fathers of the Church' the description of Jesus Christ which is called 'orthodox' emerged, to be accepted in seven great Councils of the Church between the years 325 and 787. This description of Jesus Christ was based on Paul and John but expressed in terms of a Greek philosophy which is no longer current today. What matters most in it can be put very simply in contemporary language.

Not only was the teaching of Jesus inspired by God. The whole life of Jesus was itself, from its beginning, an action by God – the action to reach and save us. The life of Jesus was the expression of God's own life in a human life. God, who is beyond space and time, has expressed himself in all that exists – but supremely he has embodied his life in a man who was born and who died, and who was raised from death.

As John put it in his first chapter, the whole business of creating the universe has been like God making a mighty speech – and in the life of Jesus Christ that Word actually 'became flesh'! For the life of God was enfleshed (which is what the Latin word behind our 'incarnate' means) – made a baby's flesh, made the flesh of a man who was hungry, weary, lonely and sorrowful, made poor flesh, made the flesh of a man who died in agony. Jesus was fully human, but the humanity of Jesus was used by God to show his love, and for this great purpose it was the perfect instrument. In the man Jesus of Nazareth, the love of God walked the earth and was nailed to wood.

That is what the life of Jesus Christ was. And that life has never ended. Certainly he lived and died in Palestine, but if we stop his biography there we cannot make sense of the experiences of countless Christians since his death. Jesus is alive today. He is our contemporary. He is near us, whatever our situation may be. We cannot see him – but that will not stop us knowing the difference which he makes to our life, in many practical ways, if we are willing to walk with him through the problems. This is what one of the first Christians experienced about Jesus (in the Revelation of John, 1:18): 'Do not be afraid. I am the first and the last, and I am the living one; for I was dead and now I am alive . . .' We can meet him, and in our own lives we can discover who he is.

CHAPTER FIVE

His Son, our Lord

The human face of God

But what difference does it make to us?

Jesus makes a very great difference to our understanding of God. People can come to believe in God as Creator and Ruler by meditating about life and about the planet and the universe – as so many people who are not Christians do. People can believe that God's character is like a good parent's. But even so, they will probably still think that God is very high above human life. The difference made by Jesus Christ is that now God is near, and can be called 'Father!' in deep love and happiness.

Amazing as this is, we human animals, who are all more or less weak, dirty and doomed to die, can feel at one with God – the old word for which is 'atonement'. We know God as Father through Jesus Christ. We meet God through the 'go-between' or 'mediator', the messenger who is trusted by both sides and the reconciler who can bring the two together. And so Christians find themselves driven by their own experience to make the Christian statement about God. This is the statement that God is not only known as Father, he is also known as Son.

Every man, woman or child ever born is, in a sense, a son or daughter of God the Father. But not everybody has lived a life such as that of Jesus of Nazareth. In fact, no one has come near to repeating that life, let alone doing better. The history of the world has not produced anyone who has made such an impact as this carpenter who was executed while still in his thirties. That is why Christians have always believed that Jesus is the Son of God in a special, utterly unique, sense. And that is why, century after century, Christians have struggled to develop theology (a word which means 'reasoning about God') in a Christian way.

Every Christian is under an obligation to think about God in that way – and think hard. For to say that Jesus Christ is the 'Word of God' means that his life is the climax of all God's creation – and the clue to the mystery of what God intends by his creation. He is the A and the Z, and now all the other letters can be arranged in order. So our understanding of the whole world is profoundly influenced if we accept the revelation of God's character and purpose in Jesus Christ. We read the newspapers with this in mind. In this light we examine any knowledge we may have of science, or economics, or psychology, or history. We see all life in the perspective given by Jesus as the way to the truth.

And we see him as the way to the truth about the eternal God. While he lived for 30 years or a bit more in Palestine, Jesus prayed to his Father, obeyed his Father, walked with his Father into all life's problems and into death. Christians have always seen in that relationship the enfleshment or 'incarnation' of a relationship which goes beyond time and space into eternity. Jesus is eternally the Son. This is the vision which has made Christians feel that it is right to pray not only to God the Father (as Jesus did in Palestine), but also to Jesus himself, in eternity. For the expression of God's creative purpose seen in this life, death and resurrection of Jesus has never stopped. The act of God's powerful love which people saw in Palestine some 2,000 years ago continues (in a different way, of course) in our own lives before we die – and also after we die.

We can go on knowing God's own creative love in him, and so we can pray through or to Jesus as a friend we can trust. He is still the messenger and the reconciler, bridging the gap which separates us from the Holy and the Eternal. For us, encountering holiness or entering eternity must be a bit like entering a royal palace or a large government office. It would be a relief to see, amid your anxiety, a brother or a friend who by a miracle is in the very same place. And for us, whether we live before or after death, Jesus Christ is the human face of God.

God loves like that

This faith in Jesus, the Word or Son of God, involves us personally – for a great difference is made to our lives if we kneel as Thomas does at the end of John's gospel and say to Jesus: 'My Lord and my God!'

The best way to see this difference is to see what the death of Jesus means to us. Often the whole life of a hero or heroine is summed up in the way he or she dies. That is supremely true in the case of Jesus. He accepted a very painful and humiliating death in Jerusalem – when he could easily have avoided any risk by living quietly in Galilee, where he had worked as a carpenter. His willingness to die shows his courage. It also shows his love for his friends. And it shows something more.

It shows the love of God in action. That love was like sunshine, making Jesus grow and work as he did – but, when Jesus was crucified, the love of God was like sunshine going through a magnifying glass. Under that strong light, paper or a leaf burns. The crucifixion of Jesus makes the strong love of God so clear that (so to speak) our hearts are set on fire.

For it is when we see Jesus patiently suffering that we realize how patient the love of God is. God has been patient with the world through the millions of years of evolution – but perhaps he has had to be more patient still with us, in the few years when we have been alive. Although God's happiness must be great beyond our understanding, we can begin to understand that the patience involved in God's chosen method of working must be similar in some ways to our own experience of suffering. As Jesus hangs on the cross dying, we begin to see that his acceptance of pain is not only the act of a brave and loving man, but is also a kind of poster, or film, which is about God's love for his whole creation and specially for humanity. God loves us so much that he wants to share what distresses us. He does not send suffering in order to punish us; he shares suffering in order to be with us, and now nothing that we undergo can be worse than God's own experience. And that moves us more than all the majestic power of God displayed in an earthquake or in the stars.

When we see Jesus on the cross, we also begin to see how terribly wrong we have been in responding, or failing to respond, to God's good purpose. Jesus was rejected and left alone – as God the Father has often been. He was treated with contempt and cruelty – and people have often behaved in the same way towards God's creation, specially towards the men and women who are God's children. When we see that happening, we know that if we had been there, we should probably have behaved as the cowardly friends of Jesus did, or as the mob did (shouting 'Hosanna' one day and 'Crucify' before the end of the week), or as Jewish priests did, or as the Roman soldiers did. The word 'sin' now has a serious meaning because when we realize what people like us did to Jesus, we know what sin does.

In the old days people pictured devils as causing sin, disease and death. In our time many people find such pictures amusing rather than frightening, and so the old pictures may fail to bring home to us the fact which lies behind them – the fact that evil is very powerful, spreading like poison in the human spirit, growing like cancer to destroy. In the old days people spoke of 'the sin of Adam'. In our time most people know that the story of Adam and Eve is not literally true – and they have forgotten that in Hebrew Adam meant 'Man' and Eve meant 'Life'. So the old words may not speak to us of the terrible power of evil. But the crucifixion of Jesus speaks. In a film or a novel the hero or heroine may have to spend time under the power of the 'baddies'. That is the test of courage in a world where evil often seems to win. The crucifixion is the time which God spent under the power of human evil.

The most wonderful thing about the cross is, however, that it makes us see that the patient love of God is stronger than the most powerful evil. For nothing – nothing at all – can defeat God's purpose, which is always to reach us in healing and forgiveness. Just as Jesus on the cross does not change in his spirit while his body dies, so God does not change. We do our worst – and God carries on being God. The whole life and death of Jesus of Nazareth shows us God taking action decisively. Jesus did not have to die to 'appease' God, as if God had taken offence and needed to be placated before he could calm down and forgive us. No, the cross 'reveals' God. The life and death of Jesus discloses to us what God is, always was and always will be. God loves like that!

There are many ways of interpreting this action by God. Many Christians have spoken of a great victory won on the cross.

Although the crucifixion must have seemed a total disaster to the followers of Jesus at the time, this Christian vision of the cross as the triumph of courageous love is a true understanding of the horror. The New Testament speaks of the willingness of Jesus to undergo crucifixion as a sacrifice which replaced the innumerable sacrifices of animals in the temples in Jerusalem and throughout the ancient world. Although we do not sacrifice animals or humans in these days, we have many myths (such as that of James Bond) in which the hero overcomes evil only at the risk of his own life. And in real life, self-sacrifice is still needed.

Many Christians have spoken of Jesus carrying the consequences of humanity's sin. When he is tortured to death as a result of sin, Jesus takes it like a boxer accepting 'punishment' in the ring. Many Christians have spoken of the death of Jesus as our 'redemption' – which means that it is like buying back someone from slavery by paying the price of freedom (the ransom). When slavery is unfamiliar, it may be more helpful to think of someone deep in debt being released from that nightmare. Many Christians have spoken of Christ as the 'substitute' for us, and he is that – like someone who goes to the rescue, plunging into fire or sea while we remain onlookers. And Christians have spoken of the appeal of the cross to our consciences. Paul wrote to the Romans: 'Christ died for us while we were yet sinners, and that is God's own proof of his love towards us' (5:8). And some Christians have spoken of the whole world being brought back to the knowledge and love of God, by seeing God in the crucified Jesus. That is what Paul wrote in his second letter to the Corinthians (5:18, 19): 'From first to last, this has been the work of God . . . God was in Christ reconciling the world to himself.'

There is a technical term which Christians use: grace. In ordinary modern speech, the word refers to attractiveness, charm and ease – specially in movement. We speak of an athlete jumping gracefully, or of a graceful dance. We are liable to forget that God is supremely attractive – and supremely generous. But when we survey the cross where Jesus died, we remember. And then we know what Paul meant when he wrote of 'the grace of our Lord Jesus Christ'.

There is another technical term in the Christian vocabulary: justification. This refers to a prisoner who is declared to be just or innocent by a merciful judge – even though the prisoner may be in fact guilty. Christians feel like this when they trust in the mercy of God after viewing the cross, when they 'believe in' God as they believe or trust in their dearest friend. That is the explanation of what Christian theology says about 'justification by grace, received through faith'.

There are many ways of defining what 'a Christian' is. The best way is this: a Christian is one who takes orders from Jesus Christ as Lord. There are many ways of defining what 'the Church' is. The best way is this: the Church is the fellowship of those who accept Jesus as Lord. And there are many ways of defining what it means to be truly and fully human. The best way is this: God took human nature to embody his own nature, and that shows the height to which human nature can rise. Those who accept and follow Jesus are acknowledged by him as his brothers and sisters; hearing God speak through him, they are united with him for ever. But everybody – whatever his or her religion, colour, nationality, income, education or beauty – is a brother or a sister in an important sense. They walk the same earth that Jesus walked. They have the same flesh. They, too, are loved by the Love which was proclaimed when the embodied God hung on a Roman instrument of deadly torture.

CHAPTER SIX

We believe in the Holy Spirit

Three in one

There is only one real God – as there is only one real universe, which is his creation. Christianity does not teach that there are three gods. But three ways have been shown to us in which God is God. First there is the way in which God makes, keeps and holds together all that exists – as Creator, Ruler and Father. Then there is the way in which God acts in patient but victorious love, in a human life – as the Son. And finally there is the Spirit. It is because Christians have had this experience that they struggle to make sense of it, just as someone who is in love tries to speak of that.

The teaching about God as the Holy Trinity has to cover the fact that Christians have experienced the glory of God in all these three ways. None of them is second-rate. So Christians believe that in each way God is being himself personally – although God is not three separate people.

Because new life has been experienced by Christians, the Spirit is believed to be given by God the Father through God the Son. And that is why Father, Son and Spirit can each be worshipped as fully divine although Christian prayer is normally offered to the Father, through the Son, in the power of the Spirit. The activity of God, as experienced by Christians, is summed up by Paul as he ends the second letter to Corinth: 'the grace of the Lord Jesus Christ, and the love of God, and fellowship in the Holy Spirit'. It is an astonishing phrase, for it shows how early in their history the Christians felt themselves compelled by their experience to speak of the Lord Jesus Christ, and of the Holy Spirit, in the same breath as they spoke of God.

A picture may – or may not – help. Perhaps the best to use is an old one although it is not in the Bible: the Father sits on the throne and uses two hands, the Son and the Spirit. In the Bible itself the activity of God is often compared both with fire and with water. The main point of the comparison is the sheer excitement of knowing that God acts – it is like suddenly seeing a fire in the dark night, or like finding water in the desert. But it may help our understanding of God's action to notice that there are three equally effective ways in which fire is fire. Fire gives warmth – fire gives light – and fire burns. There are also three equally effective ways in which water is water. Water quenches thirst – water washes – and water makes steam, which can supply the energy to run a machine. Of course these are only pictures and all of them are more or less inadequate. But often we think in pictures.

This belief that God is Three-in-One is the centre of fully Christian thinking, and it ought to alert us to the significance of God the Holy Spirit. But it is even more vital that we should have the experience which is here being talked about. For only the full Christian experience, including experience of the energy of the Holy Spirit, makes Christianity what it ought always to be: fire in the world, a torrent of living water.

God the power

What, then, does God the Holy Spirit do? The Bible gives many answers. The word 'spirit' suggests what is greatest in human activity. When someone is making her best effort, there is a phrase which is sometimes used in order to applaud: 'That's the spirit!' So whenever God is specially active, the Bible speaks about his 'Spirit'.

In the Old Testament the Spirit of God is said to have been over the waters which chaotically covered the earth in an early period (or 'day') of the earth's creation. Out of those waters life came – as modern science agrees. But God's special activity occurs most dramatically in the lives of men and women when at last they, too, are created. The Old Testament says that in many such lives the 'Spirit' is at work. The Spirit of God is said to have inspired the early heroes of Israel (the judges), the men and women who later on were Israel's guides (the prophets), Israel's rulers (the kings), and the skilled craftsmen and artists who made beautiful furnishings and robes for the temple in Jerusalem.

Here in the Bible is a vast picture of the Spirit's work. Our understanding of the world in our time – and of all the past – must not be smaller. Whenever we see something new being created by adventure, and progress being made through taking risks, and reversals being accepted in an unconquerable hope, we should say: 'There's God!' Whenever order emerges out of chaos, and life out of dull matter, and beauty out of raw material, we should say: 'That's the Spirit!' Whenever there is some outstanding ability, such as scientific ability or athletic ability, we should say: 'That's God's gift!'

But in the New Testament, a surprising new form of the Spirit's activity is reported. Here the most ordinary people, leading the most commonplace lives, are invaded, shaken and possessed by the Spirit. And all this is because of the new man – Jesus.

The new life which floods into Christians is life brought by Jesus, and the new truth which they glimpse is the truth made human in Jesus. Their new power is the power of the Holy Spirit – seen, as never before, in Jesus. Their new prayer is like having a brilliant lawyer or 'advocate' to speak up for one, saying what one could never express so well oneself – but this advocate carries on the work of Jesus.

All this is implied in the farewell speech of Jesus in John's gospel (chapter 14):

> I will ask the Father, and he will give you another, to be your Advocate, who will be with you for ever – the Spirit of truth ... Because I live, you too will live ... The Holy Spirit whom the Father will send in my name will teach you everything, and will call to mind all that I have told you.

Jesus, who was so full of the Spirit, promised that the Father would give the Spirit to those who asked, as a parent always gives food to a hungry child who asks. In Jerusalem, when for the first time after the crucifixion and resurrection of Jesus they were celebrating the Jewish harvest festival called Pentecost, this promise came true. The small company of Christians felt themselves filled with a new power. In their excitement they broke out in strange sounds and cries. They excited those around them, who then listened to the first Christian sermon. And their new power did not leave them. It gave them courage to defy the authorities. It gave them eloquence to announce their message and to argue for its truth. It gave them the power to heal many who were sick. The power of the Spirit was what took the Christian faith from Jerusalem into the whole of the world. It has had an effect rather like the arrival of electricity in a place which had depended on candles and muscles.

The Acts of the Apostles, which tells the story of this Pentecost in its second chapter, is Luke's account of how the new faith was taken from Jerusalem to Rome, where it proved stronger than the Roman Empire itself. That book shows that wherever the faith went, the promise was repeated that the Spirit would be given. And the Spirit came. God came in this new power to people of many nations and races. The same Spirit came to men and women – most of them poor and uneducated, a few of them influential and intellectually brilliant. These Christians still had many human weaknesses – but at least they knew that. Their pride was (as Paul wrote) crucified. For the Spirit always came as strength amid weakness: the weakness was human, the power was divine.

The same power has been experienced by Christians in every generation since those first days. Sometimes intense emotions have been aroused, and the ability to speak in 'strange tongues', as known at that Pentecost festival in Jerusalem, has also been known by many other Christians. Christians who specially value such gifts of the Holy Spirit can be called Pentecostalists, and there are flourishing Pentecostal Churches in the world today. When these Christians remain loyally within churches such as the Anglican Churches, they are called the 'charismatic' movement, from the Greek for 'gift', because they know that the power is still given.

But the extraordinary excitements are not the most important gifts of the Spirit. The stress has been on the quieter, perhaps longer-lasting, gifts; the Spirit's gift of love has been put first. Writing to the Galatians (5:22) Paul described the 'harvest' of the Spirit. Here it is: 'love, joy, peace, kindness, goodness, fidelity, gentleness and self-control'. People sometimes talk as if such virtues can be manufactured, or produced by human effort. But that is not the Christian experience. The reason why all these virtues are called a 'harvest' is that each of them comes from a seed, as does the wheat in the field or the apple on the tree. That seed is God's love for us. As Paul wrote to the Romans: 'God's love has flooded our inmost heart through the Holy Spirit he has given us' (5:5).

Here Christian experience corresponds with our observation of those we meet every day. We notice that people who are self-controlled, gentle, loyal, good and kind are people who, deep in themselves, are at peace and full of happiness. Those who are loving are those who have been loved – by their parents, by their friends, by their wives or husbands. Because they are assured of love, they have a relaxed and generous attitude to others. But the Christian experience is that even those who have been starved of human love can experience God's love, while those who have known the richness of human love can find that God's love is better. In all their hearts, God's Spirit can be poured out lavishly.

This, then, is the third way in which God is God. And when we know this, we are not surprised about what Christians have always said: without the good news of God the Spirit, there is no full account of the Christian message. Nor are we surprised when Christians ask each other: 'Have you, too, received the Spirit?' Christianity is sometimes presented as a series of challenges – do better, and better still! But it matters far more that this good news is a series of offers – you need it, so here is strength.

CHAPTER SEVEN

We believe in love

This is sex . . .

Everyone wants to be loved. We rely on the support and approval of our friends. Sex is a big part of human nature, and most of us need the special warmth and companionship of the girlfriend or the boyfriend, the wife or the husband. We also need the security of a loving home, with a family life based on the rock-like foundation of a stable marriage. Without such love, we can feel lonely and lost. A modern Anglican poet, W. H. Auden, summed up everything:

> Space is the Whom our loves are needed by,
> Time is our choice of How to love and why.

But what is 'love'? Obviously, sex is often a vehicle for love. And it is equally obvious that many people think that Christians are unaware of this. Many people suppose that Christianity takes an entirely negative attitude to sex. So it is best to be frank. The Bible's attitude to sex is positive; indeed, the Song of Songs in the Old Testament is beautifully erotic. Jesus never refused to have anything to do with people who sinned sexually; the gospels are clear about that. No one should make sex a reason for giving up prayer or for staying away from the Church.

In the Bible and in almost all the history of the Church the teaching is clear and firm: there should be no sexual intercourse outside the marriage of one man with one woman. Although in the Old Testament a man is allowed to divorce his wife, in the New Testament the teaching of Jesus (Mark 10:1–9) is definite that a man should be faithful to his wife until death, as 'one flesh'. (Under ancient Jewish law, no provision was made for a wife to initiate a divorce, although this seems to have happened sometimes.) And today many people still believe that this is the only standard of sexual behaviour which deserves to be called truly Christian. Usually there is a charitable attitude toward individuals who have not been able to live up to this standard, but there is also a conviction that the Church as a whole ought to be loyal to what has been clearly stated in the Bible and by the Church itself in the past. There is certainty that only this teaching can show that marriage is the right place for sexual activity in God's plan.

Why, then, is this traditional morality being questioned by many Christians in our own time? The answer which is often given is that there has been a decline in sexual morality which has infected Christians as well as the societies around them – but, it is added, this is no reason why the Christian Church should feel free to change its position. Indeed, it is hoped that the faithfulness of the Church to the Bible will set an example which will encourage faithfulness and happiness within marriage, to the great benefit of children and of society as a whole.

But in recent years many Christians have not been persuaded that this answer is all that needs to be said, and several reasons can be given. One is that Jesus was holding up an ideal, teaching how people ought to behave in the kingdom of God, not laying down a law which allows no exceptions. For example, in the Sermon on the Mount (Matthew 5:31, 32) an exception to the teaching against divorce is made when a husband finds that his wife has been 'unchaste', which almost certainly refers to adultery. In his first letter to the Christians in Corinth (7:10–16) Paul repeats the teaching of Jesus that divorce is always wrong but advises a Christian to accept a separation when his or her partner wishes neither to become a Christian nor to continue the marriage. In that sad case the Christian is no longer 'bound' by the marriage, and divorce can be the lesser of two evils, because 'God's call is a call to live in peace'. And since the New Testament makes such allowances when there have been human tragedies, it can be argued that the Church today ought not to stick to a rigid line in all circumstances.

It can also be said that circumstances have changed substantially since the Bible was written and since the Church's tradition was formed. In biblical times and much later, most women were married when they were young, in the hope that they would have many children before their own lives ended at an age which we would regard as young; and women were subject to the authority first of their fathers and then of their husbands. But in modern society marriage usually comes later in life, after years when men and women have been ready for marriage physically and emotionally, and though marriage has been beginning later than was normal in earlier ages it usually lasts longer – perhaps for half a century – because people have longer lives. Women and men have become much more equal, and are able to survive financially (however difficult life may become) even if divorced. So it can be held that more allowances ought to be made for young people who feel sexual urges very strongly before they feel able to marry – and for older people who find that their marriages 'die' in emotional reality, before their bodies die.

The existence of almost completely reliable contraception has also challenged one very strong argument for confining sex to marriage. The possibility of producing a child made sexual intercourse a heavy responsibility for people down the ages until the late twentieth century. Although most Christians believe that sex is still an act which is full of responsibility for the happiness and self-respect of both parties, many see that the availability of almost completely reliable contraception does make serious changes in the weight and type of responsibility which rests on sexual partners.

There is also the question about whether the total condemnation of homosexual practice ought to be revised in the light of modern knowledge. It is now known that homosexuality is natural for a minority of men and women, either from birth or from an early age, and that when people experience no natural attraction to the other sex they cannot usually be altered by medical treatment. And so it can be held that not all homosexuals ought to be expected to live without a partner, any more than it is reasonable to expect all other people to live a celibate ('no sex') life.

But there is no argument which deserves to be called Christian in favour of promiscuity, which uses other people's bodies for short thrills without any intention of forming a long-lasting relationship. Such behaviour is contrary to the Christian belief that our bodies are given to us by God in order that they may be instruments of genuine love.

To be honest, we have to observe that there is this disagreement about how the teaching of the Bible and of the Church's tradition ought to be applied to people who live in a situation which is different, although not totally different. In practice Anglicans have to obey their consciences – but that does not mean 'Do what you want to do at this moment'! All Christians are agreed about some vitally important points. Whatever may be the nature of their sexuality, and whether or not they are married, everyone ought to be controlled by the principle that sex is meant to serve true and faithful love. Everyone ought to be sensitive to the feelings of other people and no one ought to engage in any activity to which a partner has not given free, glad and maturely considered agreement. Everyone ought to avoid loveless promiscuity. And everyone ought to agree that the use of sex which gives most joy to most people is when it is the physical basis of lifelong marriage, preferably growing in love with each year which passes and preferably providing a stable and happy home for children.

Those who are married begin to learn, far more deeply than they ever knew before, what love means. Here are some of the words of the traditional marriage service in church:

> I take thee to my wedded wife, to have and to hold from this day forward, for better, for worse, for richer, for poorer, in sickness and in health; to love and to cherish, till death us do part . . . With this ring I thee wed; with my body I thee honour; and all my worldly goods with thee I share . . .

When other words are used, they have the same essential meaning.

A marriage becomes strong as both husband and wife learn to put up with each other's faults and to make each other happy. They become content to sacrifice their own inclinations. Marriage is a steady giving – and it is often hard work. But it is also the most marvellous getting, for the love which is given in marriage is returned – and more. It is the best kind of friendship there is, and no other happiness in this life matches it. Marriage is always changing slightly as time marches on. For example, nowadays it is normal for wives to work outside the home if they want to or need to, before and after – or even during – the years given to looking after the children. The challenge is how to balance the job with home life – and that challenge comes to husbands too. The secret of a happy marriage is always the same: the conquest of selfishness.

. . . and this is happiness

Many advertisements pretend that if you buy something they want to sell, you will be happy. And obviously we all need not only bread but also some other things: we need them physically or emotionally. (It would be interesting to make a list of what you need!) Obviously, too, we all like jam on the bread. Many things are luxuries, but we can buy them with a reasonably clear conscience if we have earned the money.

However, the fact – not the theory, but the fact – is that happiness does not consist of the number of things we possess. We are often told that we need luxurious furniture, food and clothes, as advertised in the glossy magazines. We are also told that we need drugs including tobacco. And obviously some of these things are fun – in sensible quantities, at prices we can afford. But it is nonsense for the advertisers to promise us happiness in exchange for our money. The things that we actually need do not make a very long list and if we become obsessed with shopping for more and more possessions, that can make us the slaves of the shops even if it doesn't get us into debt. And we don't actually need the drugs which damage us. In order to relax, we don't need to let tobacco cause cancer. In order to have fun, we don't need the illegal drugs which are in fact poison. Alcohol and gambling can give us pleasure, but if we feel that we need those drugs in unreasonable amounts our lives can be wrecked. These things are often said – but a Christian has a special reason for saying them. Already God has given us (without any charge) a body more wonderful than anything else in all the world, a brain which can be more useful than any computer, and the ability to be happy without depending on any drug.

The truth is that happiness is much more likely to be found in the mind than in what our money can buy. To learn the secret of happiness, we have to understand the laws which govern our emotions.

One of these laws is that we are happy when we drown our worries in doing something we enjoy. Each of us has worries, and they are often about how we appear in the mirror or what people think of us. We have many reasons for condemning ourselves – or being sorry for ourselves. Brooding on these worries gets us nowhere, except perhaps to hell; for 'hell' is self-centred despair. We shall not be happy unless we take a holiday from ourselves, and the easiest way of doing that is to throw ourselves into an activity – which may be doing a job, or playing a game, or cooking, or going for a run, or reading, or pretty well anything that demands our attention.

We all know that it is usually more fun to do things with other people. But this doesn't apply only to a family or to a team at sport or to a party of young people. Many older people enjoy their jobs largely because of the friends they find at work – and people who are not out at work miss the companionship as well as the money. Friendship is very obviously the best road to happiness.

Many people, especially young people, become miserable, locked in the prison of the self, because they don't think they are popular. But if so, we are like prisoners with keys in our hands! For we make friends by being friendly. On the whole, people think about us precisely as we think about them. If we dislike them, they adopt the same attitude. If deep down we can't be bothered with them, they won't cross the street to meet us. It is only when we give that we receive. It is those who give love who get it back.

So if we ask 'How can I make myself more attractive?' we ought to notice that the really attractive person is usually the one who takes a real interest in other people. People who feel sorry for themselves probably need to go out and get to know someone with far greater problems, who will teach us what courage and happiness mean – and will richly repay any friendship we can offer.

When Jesus was challenged to sum up the whole of the moral

teaching of the Bible as he knew it, he did not hesitate. He quoted (from Leviticus 19:18): 'Love your neighbour as yourself.' Originally that seems to have meant: 'Stick by your fellow-Jew.' But the story of the good Samaritan (Luke 10:27–37) shows that Jesus gave a new depth of meaning to this old commandment. He did not criticize people for loving themselves, but he urged them to see how to be really happy. He was asked 'Who is my neighbour?' by someone who wanted a list of categories of people to be treated decently, but the story which he gave as an answer was a story about a Jew needing help from a Samaritan – and getting it, by the simple but often difficult action of one human being helping another. Truly to love yourself, truly to know yourself, is to see that you really do need to love other people, being to them as affectionate, as forgiving and as practical as you are to yourself. And if you treat them like that, you are likely to find that they become good neighbours to you, able and willing to help.

Some teaching by Jesus was recorded outside the gospels: 'Happiness lies more in giving than in receiving' (Acts 20:35). And the only saying of Jesus to be recorded in all four gospels is the warning that the man who saves his life will lose it. Fight your neighbour, and he will fight back! Love, and you will be loved! Fight to keep your self-centredness in your own private life, fight in order to get as much as you can, and you will never know happiness! But give your life to your neighbour, give your life away in love, and you will notice that you are happy when you are too busy to worry about it! That is the secret which Jesus tells.

In his first letter to the Corinthians (chapter 13), Paul created an unforgettable portrait of Jesus Christ – and of the true Christian. It is the portrait of a person who has found what love can do.

> Love is patient, love is kind and envies no one. Love is never boastful, nor conceited, nor rude, never selfish, not quick to take offence. Love keeps no score of wrongs; does not gloat over men's sins, but delights in the truth. There is nothing love cannot face; there is no limit to its faith, its hope, and its endurance.

Rightly, that description of love is one of the most popular parts of the Bible. What has been said so far is, however, not the full Christian understanding of love. The command to treat other people as we wish to be treated if we were in their shoes is known as the 'golden rule' and it is given in the Bible. But the Bible says much more.

The Bible shows that to believe in love is to trust in the power of love. It is to act in the conviction that love will in the end find a way and win through. So many other things seem more immediately attractive than true love, and in this chapter we have already mentioned some of them – sex for kicks, possessions, drugs. But to believe in love is to say that true love is the most valuable, the most satisfying and the most glorious experience in life. It is to say that here is gold – and in the last analysis the rest is bogus. So many other things seem more powerful than love. Violence often does. Aggressive argument often does. But to believe in love is like expecting a great river to flow into the sea. You trust love to win through because it is the mightiest force, the most dynamic energy, in the universe.

How can we believe that? It is never easy. In fact, it is only possible if we believe in God the Father – for only if God is real and loving is love more real than the other things. And Christians are those who believe in God as Father because they have seen the Father's love triumphant in the life, death and victory of Jesus, his Son our Lord. This Christians believe because they have been touched by the power of the Spirit. What this chapter has said about love is based, for the Christian, on what previous chapters have said about God.

CHAPTER EIGHT

We believe in forgiveness

We can be forgiven . . .

Everyone wants to stop pretending. We are all failures, and pretending to be successful is a burden. We try to cover up our weaknesses, but even if we deceive others we can't convince ourselves. Particularly do we feel this when we measure ourselves in comparison with the highest standards of love. Our lives are seen to be really sordid when we look at them honestly in the light of that ideal.

Even if we are blind to these facts about our own lives, the state of the world (as this is brought home to us by TV and the papers) is almost bound to make us conscious of the failures of human nature. Instead of co-operating in constructive tasks, groups spend their energies in rivalries which are often bitter. Instead of treating this planet with the respect it deserves, people behave like birds fouling their own nest. Instead of combining to grow and distribute food for all, some people on this small planet worry about slimming while others are starving. Although the danger of using nuclear, biological and chemical weapons of mass destruction is less than it used to be, the danger has not vanished. Wars and massacres have continued. Anyone who is at all sensitive to what is going on in his or her own mind, or the world around, knows why guilt features so prominently in most religions – and why the human instinct is to hope that a God exists who will listen to the prayer, 'Lord, have mercy!'

An old prayer says to the Lord Jesus Christ: 'you take away the sin of the world'. It is almost as if we were thinking about a great bulldozer clearing away the ruins of a building and all the mud and muck. When we begin, we are burdened by our many failures as individuals and as the human race. When the bulldozer has finished, it has removed the whole mess so that it can be forgotten. And when we begin again to make the mess, it begins again to take it away.

What Jesus does here is to express God's mercy in action. Supremely he did this when he continued to embody love despite the loneliness and pain of his death, praying: 'Father, forgive them: they do not know what they are doing.' But frequently this happened as he walked around Palestine. He would meet someone paralysed in spirit and in body – someone unable to move because the burden of failure and guilt was so heavy. Then Jesus would speak and act. And that person would be free, a whole person instead of a cripple. Often in his teaching Jesus would explain what was happening. It was as if a son was going back to his father after making mistakes. That son would begin to say: 'Father . . . I am no longer fit to be called your son . . .' But the father would interrupt his confession of guilt, saying to his servants: 'Quick! fetch a robe, my best one, and put it on him; put a ring on his finger and shoes on his feet . . . and let us have a feast to celebrate the day.' And even before that son had said a word to show that he was sorry, the father would run to meet him, would fling his arms round him, and would kiss him (Luke 15:11–32).

Why? Simply and solely because that boy was his father's son – whatever he had done wrong. The Christian commentary on human nature is never entirely gloomy. Christianity says that the human being is a sinner, in case we haven't read as much in today's paper. But Christianity quickly adds that the human being is also a creature of great dignity and value, an animal with unique skills and powers, a marvellous and beautiful being with almost unlimited opportunities, already full of goodness, the child of God and in many ways like the Father. So the Father sees. The Father cares. The Father runs. And the Father welcomes home.

But if God is best compared with a loving parent, we may ask why he is also compared with a judge. The answer, surely, is known by everyone who has ever had a truly loving parent. Wanting the best for the child is part of love – and so is the wish to show what is best, by talking about it, by protests when the child fails to reach it, and by correction involving discipline and sometimes punishment. A child who is punished may feel for a time that the parent is an enemy, but that is a misunderstanding. The parent's love does not cease when it is not soft. And the parent is far happier when forgiving than when being strict.

According to the teaching of Jesus, God's forgiveness is offered to all – on two conditions only. We often read with interest the advertisements which say 'A free gift!' and add one or two conditions. How much more should we notice the conditions which are attached to the offer to take away the sin of the world! And these conditions are not merely snags attached to a free offer. They state firmly how we must react if we are able to receive God's free offer of total forgiveness.

The first condition is that we should mean what we say when we say that we are sorry. The reason why this is necessary is that unless we are really open to receive what God offers we cannot experience the forgiveness and the newness of life. If we do not mean our 'Sorry', it is like saying 'Welcome' to a guest – and keeping the front door closed. God will not force himself on us. God will not break down the door if we decide to keep it shut. God keeps on knocking, but he values our freedom so much that he allows the door to be locked on the inside – and he continues to allow this even when his constant knocking makes him bleed. This amazing attitude on the part of God ought to be matched in our own relationships with other humans. We can be ready to forgive, and we must be – although the process of forgiveness will not be complete if the other person does not accept what we can offer and does not offer forgiveness for any harm which we may have done.

Because Jesus insisted on reality and honesty in our relationships with each other and with God, he warned his hearers very solemnly that 'if anyone speaks against the Holy Spirit, for him there is no forgiveness'. This means that if anyone does not accept that good is good and that truth is truth, he or she cannot be shown the truth and cannot be strengthened in goodness. As the twelfth chapter of Matthew's gospel explains, the warning comes when some of the enemies of Jesus have sneered at his work of healing people, saying that it was inspired by 'Beelzebub the prince of devils'.

The second condition attached to God's offer of forgiveness is expressed in the prayer which Jesus gave to his followers: 'Forgive us our sins as we are willing to forgive those who sin against us!' This means that we cannot ask for God's forgiveness except to the extent that we forgive those who have wronged us. If we love and forgive others only a little, we shall be forgiven by God only a little; if we are totally unforgiving, we shall be totally unforgiven. (Jesus warned us of our spiritual danger by telling the story of the man whose debt running into millions was wiped out at a stroke by an extraordinarily generous king. That man left the king and immediately demanded that a fellow-servant should repay him a debt amounting to only a small sum. When the king heard about that cruel unfairness, he insisted that the scoundrel should pay him back every bit.) But the reason for this second condition is the same as for the first. If we are ungenerous to others, it shows that we do not really understand that God is being generous to us, and so we are not able to accept God's free offer. We are still hoping to defend the old life of selfishness; we cannot let ourselves be invaded by the new life.

If we understand this second condition attached to God's offer, what we have to do is to think of those we most dislike – and pray to God, 'Lord forgive me to the precise extent that I am willing to forgive that person!' And obviously this includes people whom we dislike because of our prejudices about colour, nationality, class or religion. We have to acknowledge one and all as human – like ourselves. Just as sinful! But just as lovable! When we trust in God's forgiveness, it is because we believe that he understands why his children have such weaknesses. He knows what difficult circumstances we face, what fierce temptations we undergo; he knows our difficulties, because he knows us. But that is the way in which we have to see our brother or our sister – to understand, and to forgive.

Anyone can receive God's forgiveness by asking God sincerely for it – if he or she is firmly resolved to live in love and peace with all. But the Church makes available to us, if we want it, an additional privilege. If we wish to confess our sins out loud before a priest, the priest can advise us about any problems and can assure us of God's forgiveness. Any priest of the Church of England is authorized to hear a confession, and is bound to treat it as absolutely private and confidential. The practice is not compulsory in the Church of England – but the Church provides this privilege, and it can be a great blessing.

. . . for ever

It only remains to be added that neither the warning nor the offer announced by Jesus is cancelled by death. It is very difficult indeed to use any pictures or words about what lies beyond death, for all the pictures or words which are available refer to life before death. All we can say is this: if we are what Christianity says we are – not only sinners but also unique, beautiful and good, the children of God – then God the Father will not throw us away when we die like a smoker throwing away the end of a cigarette. What the Bible calls 'eternal life' begins here and now, but it is not brought to an end by the death of the body.

There is a grim side to the teaching of Jesus about life after death, for often in the gospels Jesus warns us that the eternal God will still attach those two conditions to his free offer when we have died. If we are to live with God in his glory, we must ourselves be willing to say 'Yes' to him. And we must be willing to live in love. In eternity any possibility of life for us can no longer be based on our possession of the bodies which have died: it must depend entirely on being willing to share the eternal life of God, the God who keeps us alive because he loves.

Jesus speaks about hell, using the traditional pictures familiar to his hearers (pictures of perpetual fires and horrid worms, derived from the smouldering rubbish dump in the valley outside Jerusalem). What 'hell' means is saying 'No' to God, preferring darkness to light, hatred to love, death to life. Jesus warns that this ruin, this destruction, which can be pointed to by using the images of exclusion, death and horror, is a terrible possibility. But it is also possible that everyone will in the end choose God, light, love and life. Indeed, many Christians believe that this will be the end of the human story – and all Christians hope so.

'Heaven' is God's forgiveness in eternity. The pictures of angels, harps, jewels and gold cannot be true literally, for the reality of what is beyond space and time, in God's own life, must be more splendid than any pictures or words. But these pictures, and the great words still used in Christian worship, can point to the reality as the small model may give an idea of the big ship. A promise about heaven is that, out of what he has himself made, God will make the best that is possible to him. Our essential personalities will remain because these are what God loves, but we shall be changed gloriously. Christians who believe in God, and pray to him, and try to obey him in their lives, are confident of God's future because of what they have learned about God already. They have glimpsed God's glory, and this makes them hope for the vision of God as he really is in his eternal perfection. They have experienced God's faithfulness and loyalty in their lives, and this makes them long to know God's full love.

We know almost nothing about heaven. But if you believe that God is real, and is your loving Father, then you can know that he will keep you in eternal life – it will be the same you! And if you believe that God is eternal, and is holy and perfect, then you can know that you will have to be changed in order to share his life and his glory – it will be a completely grown-up you! And what you hope for yourself you can hope for those who are dear to you, and for everyone.

If this is the reality behind our pictures of heaven, then the hope of reaching it is a great hope inspiring our present struggles. Those whom we call 'saints' are those who, we believe, have been made perfect by God in heaven. We believe this because already before death their lives were special. They were not perfect then, but they showed so many signs of being in touch with God that they help us to trust in God's wisdom and power.

The thought that saints in heaven can be made out of people like us is gloriously encouraging – a point made in the New Testament by using two comparisons with athletics in Ancient Greece.

At the sports, a runner who won a race would be crowned with a wreath made of leaves, and in his first letter to the Christians in Corinth (9:24–26) Paul urged them to aim at a far more valuable prize. 'At the sports all the runners run the race, though only one wins the prize. Like them, run to win! But every athlete goes into strict training. They do it to obtain a fading wreath; we, a wreath that never fades.'

In the letter to Hebrews (chapter 12), the victorious heroes of faith are compared with the spectators who shout encouragement to the competitors at the sports. So we must 'run with determination the race for which we are entered, our eyes fixed on Jesus'. If some favourite sin of ours is hindering us like an overcoat on a runner, we must stop clinging to it. We must throw it away, as an athlete removes everyday clothes in order to be free.

CHAPTER NINE

We believe in freedom

A free people

Everyone wants to be free. A great part of the history of the twentieth century consisted of the struggle of peoples to be liberated from empires – and from tyrannical governments in their own countries. A cry for freedom has started off the roar of many revolutions. But the history we inherit is also the story of a psychological liberation. People rebel against being told what to think and what to do. They demand freedom to work out their own beliefs, to vote for their own preferences, to decide how they choose to live, to behave as they think right. In many periods of history young people have rejected the merely conventional – but they are doing it with greater power today, because their revolt chimes in with the general passion for freedom.

Religion is often said to be the enemy of freedom. We are told that churches and other religious bodies have got themselves identified with imperialism and with oppressive governments. We are told that religion is itself 'opium for the people', a drug used by oppressors to distract people from their just grievances. We are told that preachers become censors when they get the chance, and that religion tries to strangle the free life of the mind and the heart.

Nowadays any honest reply to this criticism of religion has to begin by admitting with sorrow and shame that much of the criticism is true. Religion has often been used by those who have oppressed and exploited others. But Christians would now agree that this was tragically wrong. The persecutions of heretics which in the past were officially sponsored both by the Roman Catholics and by the Protestants are now condemned throughout the

Christian Church. Christians now reject the kind of mixture of religion and politics that led to the Church of England being so much under the thumb of Tudor monarchs such as Elizabeth I while Roman Catholics were put to death as traitors. Also notorious is the Inquisition set up in the Middle Ages, when the persecution of the 'heretics' would result in them being burned alive: that was seen in England during the reign of Elizabeth's Roman Catholic sister Mary. Everywhere it is now acknowledged that the only right policy is religious liberty, and that the Church's role in society is to be a servant not a lord, the pioneer of authentic love rather than the tool of power politics.

The real question is whether Christianity is essentially hostile to freedom. And the answer shouts at us from the Bible. John's gospel (8:32) contains the promise: 'You shall know the truth, and the truth will set you free.' In other words, Christianity originally did not rely on any support offered by the state or by 'respectable' opinion. In the days when it was being persecuted, and was rejected by the respectable, Christianity simply relied on being true – and the way by which people were to know its truth was by finding out for themselves its liberating power.

One of the earliest documents included in the New Testament is Paul's letter to the Galatians. One great theme of that letter is freedom. 'Christ set us free, to be free people' (5:1). The same theme runs through Paul's other teaching. For example, his second letter to the Corinthians proclaims that 'where the Spirit of the Lord is, there is liberty' (3:17).

Paul – like Jesus himself – contrasted this new freedom with the burden of trying to keep all the laws of strict Jewish religion. But the original freedom in Christianity should also be contrasted with the claims of some Christian teachers. For example, in the Middle Ages the Church did its utmost to insist on certain beliefs and practices. These were nowhere to be found in the Bible, yet they were claimed to be essential. The sixteenth century saw the 'Protestant' protest against all this. In our time the bitter controversies of the sixteenth century are dead almost everywhere. But while Protestantism has changed as Roman Catholicism has done, one kind of protest is permanently valid. Anyone who wishes to be loyal to the Christianity of the New Testament always has to protest against any attempt to substitute a man-made code of discipline, in belief or behaviour, for the original Christian freedom.

A religion is effective when it is thought to be true. And you can think it is true when – and only when – you are free to make up your own mind about it. A compulsory acceptance of orthodoxy is not genuine acceptance. To decide, each individual has to use his or her own intelligence, store of knowledge, and moral sense. It is not claimed that either the reason or the conscience is infallible, but in no other way can the individual be convinced. Truth breathes in the air of liberty.

A careful reading of the New Testament shows great differences among the people first called by Jesus to follow him. It also shows a considerable variety of outlook among Christians and among Christian congregations. One result is that there are four gospels, not one – and if you go through them carefully, you will surely notice many differences. If you read a letter by Paul, and then the letter of James, you might be forgiven for wondering whether the same religion is being described. In Paul's letter to the Galatians, he recalls a fierce argument with Peter: 'I opposed him to his face, because he was clearly in the wrong' (2:11). The religion of the New Testament was not uniform, and there is no good reason why Christianity today should be.

Sometimes it is claimed that the Bible is infallible (no error is possible) or that it is 'inerrant' (containing no error). This claim may provoke the equally crude reply that the Bible is 'untrue' or 'a lot of fairy stories'. Actually the Bible which Christians accept consists of 66 books written over a period of about a thousand years. Its material varies from Hebrew folk-tales handed on over many hundreds of years to letters dictated by Paul in response to a crisis in a church; from laws designed for an ancient people to poems which are timeless in their emotional intimacy but very varied in their moods. There is no need to claim that all this material is equally 'true'; indeed, when related to the actual material in the Bible such a generalization is so sweeping that it scarcely makes sense. But it is surely also wrong to say that this material nowhere touches reality. What is true, and therefore authoritative, for the Christian is what is taught by the Bible when the Christian Bible is taken as a whole and taken together with modern knowledge (not necessarily with modern opinion) –

and this message comes out much more clearly from the New Testament than from the Old. The heart of the message is the good news about Jesus Christ. All Christian doctrine is a commentary on that news. All Christian behaviour is the result of hearing that news. But it is legitimate for Christians to comment and to behave in more than one way.

Does this mean that truth is never established, that sufficient agreement is never reached about what is true or false, right or wrong? Not at all! The New Testament is in favour neither of intellectual laziness nor of practical chaos.

What happens in the Church, as in any other free and healthy society, is that much agreement can be reached by a slow process of careful thought and free debate, with continuing prayer since this is a Church. It is for this reason that the Church of England (for example) arranges for each congregation to meet for business at least once a year, and for the day-to-day life of the Church to be settled after free discussion in the Parochial Church Council and in various higher councils or 'synods'. But even when a majority has been reached, individuals who disagree are not expelled or punished, unless the departure from what seems essential in belief or behaviour is very great.

Does this mean that every slogan is sacred, or that the purpose of church life is to provide an audience to hear everybody ventilate his or her own pet theories? Not at all! The New Testament attacks the stupid kind of ignorant pride that begins: 'What I always say is . . .' But equally, it rebukes the kind of cowardice which never moves unless the crowd moves.

We are all familiar with the fact that sincere religion can do more than anything else to rescue someone from the destructive forms of sex, alcohol, drugs or gambling; from contact with a power greater than himself or herself, someone who had been the slave of a health-wrecking habit gets the strength needed to break free. But it is also a fact that in less dramatic ways religion can liberate the mind, for someone who is open to what God wants is delivered from slavery to fashion. There are fashionable opinions just as there are fashionable clothes – and one's mind can be chained to the latest trend. 'Everybody does it' or 'My friends all say so' or 'It was in that paperback' or 'It was on TV' or 'It's the "in" thing' is often said, but it is just not a good enough reason why a Christian should agree. Humility under the true God – the God who leads us into every kind of truth – frees a Christian from depending on the crowd's applause.

Personal liberation

Christianity can make a big improvement in people's dealings with each other, freeing them from pride and cowardice. But Christianity is even more interested in the thoughts which people have when they are on their own. Pride itself may be an attempt to conceal a deep insecurity. Many of us when alone have to wrestle with emotions which carry no prestige – worries, deep anxiety, regrets, guilt, shame, loneliness, a fear that we have been rejected, a sense that our lives are futile and meaningless. The fact that many people when alone feel close to despair is one of the main reasons why so many people need tranquillizers or are mentally sick, amid the luxuries of an affluent society. It is not a new fact – these emotions have always been part of being human. And to us in this condition, freedom has been announced.

The New Testament's teaching that we are 'ransomed' from 'sin' by the 'blood' of Christ may seem remote from our age, but actually it is that offer many are looking for. 'Ransomed' means liberated. In our time kidnapped people are freed when a ransom has been paid; we can think of the delight of someone who has been deep in debt but is suddenly given the money which ends that nightmare. 'Sin' means everything in us that refuses to accept our own proper dignity in the home of God our Father. The 'blood' of Christ means his life, poured out in love. So the Christian message is that we are liberated from every kind of captivity, freed into the life with God through life with or 'in' Christ.

This message offers personal liberation at a level deeper than politics – and the offer was never needed more than in our time, when millions of people who are 'free' (and who in many cases have money and privileges enough and to spare) still feel imprisoned in the cage created for the human spirit by materialism and selfishness. So many of us today are like people who, on release from one prison, immediately head for another – just to be with other prisoners. Christianity calls out each individual to stand undressed before the cleansing forgiveness of God, as a solitary swimmer can stand on the beach at the edge of the sea.

That is why everyone is challenged to respond to God through Jesus Christ in a personal turning (which is what the word 'conversion' means). You have to meet Jesus yourself, and to accept him as your friend and as your Lord. You must be able to say for yourself that you believe in him. As Paul's second letter to Timothy (1.12) puts it: 'I know who it is in whom I have trusted.' The service of Baptism is a turning point of the utmost importance, for in it a question is put. It is very simple, but very searching. 'Do you turn to Christ as Saviour? Do you submit to Christ as Lord? Do you come to Christ, the way, the truth and the life?' And the Christian is the one who answers 'Yes'. If the cost seems too great, remember what the old prayer says – to serve God is 'perfect freedom'.

In many Christian lives, this turning or conversion reaches a climax which can be dated. People can remember the exact time when they accepted Jesus Christ as Lord and Liberator, often after intense struggles to escape from the pressure of his love. But it is not necessary to be able to date your conversion like that. Other Christians reached the position which they now occupy quietly and gradually, without any great conflict in their emotions and without any decisive crisis.

What is essential is that everyone should have his or her own personal reasons for being a Christian. You cannot inherit Christian faith as you can inherit red hair or a peculiar nose. You cannot copy Christian faith as you can copy a hair-style or an accent. And you cannot get it completely out of books, as you can get a knowledge of history. Your faith, to be authentic, to guide your life, must be your own. Your very own experience, whether it is dramatic or quiet, long or short, must lead you to know Jesus Christ as your personal Liberator.

It is instructive to read through the first ten chapters of Mark's gospel (for example), noting how personal were the demand and the offer made by the Liberator. To Simon Peter and Andrew: 'Come with me, and I will make you fishers of men.' To a man with a bad skin disease: 'Be clean again!' To a man who seemed paralysed: 'Stand up, take your bed, and go home.' To a tax-collector: 'Follow me.' To a man with a withered arm: 'Stretch out your arm.' To a man convulsed in fits: 'What is your name?' To a woman in a crowd: 'My daughter, your faith has cured you.' To a little girl apparently dead: 'Get up, my child.' To his disciples: 'And you, who do you say that I am?' To all the people: 'Anyone who wishes to be a follower of mine must leave self behind, he must take up his cross, and come with me. Whoever cares for his own safety is lost, but whoever lets himself be lost for my sake and for the Gospel, is safe. What does a man gain by winning the whole world at the cost of his life?' To the father of a boy who seemed mad: 'Everything is possible to the one who has faith.' And to a rich young man who was dissatisfied: 'One thing you lack: go, sell everything you have, and give to the poor, and you will have riches in heaven, and come, follow me.'

There have been countless women among the friends of Jesus. It is interesting how different are the women who come into personal contact with Jesus in the first ten chapters of Luke's gospel: his own mother Mary, and Elizabeth her cousin, Anna in her eighties, Simon Peter's mother-in-law who is ill in bed, the widow grieving for her son in Nain, Mary of Magdala 'from whom seven devils had come out', Joanna the wife of an official at Herod's court, Susanna and many others, Martha so busy with the cooking, Mary her quietly attentive sister. The personality of Jesus must have made an enormous impact on all these women. The gospels say that many women followed him on his journeys and were welcome to listen to his teaching – and that some women financed the work. All this is in contrast with the conventions that women had no permission to be in close contact with a religious teacher.

We are also told that Jesus was criticized for being friendly with prostitutes (mostly women divorced by their husbands, often unjustly); to them, too, he gave the message of the Father's love. And many generations have been moved and inspired by the relationship between Jesus and the 'Blessed Virgin' who had been chosen in God's plan to be his mother. They were a large family in the village of Nazareth, for Jesus had many brothers and sisters, and as would be expected the family found it hard to understand him when he left his job as a carpenter for his mission. We are told that his mother joined his brothers in protest. But she could not cut him out of her life, and in the Acts of the Apostles we find her among the first Christians. Mary had been prepared by God to be worthy to be his mother; now she was his disciple, and multitudes of Christians have loved (not worshipped!) her as the 'Mother of God' and the 'Mother of the Church'. No wonder that Luke tells us (24:10) that some women stayed with Jesus until his death and burial – 'Mary of Magdala, Joanna, and Mary the mother of Jesus, with the other women'! And no wonder that in the fourth gospel Mary of Magdala is the first person to whom Jesus reveals the glory of his resurrection!

At the end of John's gospel Jesus asks Simon Peter: 'Do you love me?' Very simply Peter replies: 'Lord, you know I love you.' So he hears the command of the Lord: 'Follow me.' He has made his free decision.

CHAPTER TEN

We believe in listening

To pray is to listen

Usually we don't really listen. Radio or TV is a background noise. We meet too many people to think it possible to listen to what they are saying with the kind of attention that catches what they mean but can't say. But many of us want more peace in order to listen more. Sometimes we have listened to music – or to friends sharing their secrets. There have even been times when we have listened to trees – or to silence. Those were moments when we were freed from the noisy, futile roundabout of our own worries, desires and jealousies.

People who patiently practise it find prayer to be the best, most instructive, most calming, encouraging and liberating kind of listening.

The trouble is that so many people with only a superficial knowledge of prayer think that it is mostly talking. Indeed, they sometimes seem to think that it consists of sleepily repeating the formula: 'God-bless-Mum-and-Dad-and-make-me-a-good-boy/girl.' To such people prayer, even when it is made in adult language, is like telephoning. One pours out many apologies and explanations about oneself, then one produces a long shopping list of things one wants. A phone call like that is so full of our own noise that we doubt whether there is anyone listening at the other end – particularly when we count the things that arrive and find that they aren't exactly what we ordered.

Real prayer is listening to God. The first essential is to 'shut the door', as Jesus put it. The world is very busy, agitating our feelings and exhausting our energies – but here and now, as we begin real prayer, we deliberately shut the world out. I am so deeply interested in myself and in how special I am that I can't decide quite what is most interesting about me – but here and now, as I turn to God, I deliberately forget myself. This is to be a journey inwards, but not in order to talk to myself. Real prayer begins by concentrating on God. And often it can usefully end there.

There is an ancient phrase still used in Christian worship: 'Lift up your hearts!' We have to let ourselves rise to the greatness of God – almost as an astronaut has to be lifted into space. We enjoy spending time with someone we love; we enjoy just being silent, together. Now we are with God! In the stillness is power, peace, love! But most people find it difficult to use abstract ideas in order to get near God. You may be helped more by looking at a reproduction of a painting, or at a flower. Best of all, gaze on the beauty of God by using the picture of himself which he has supplied: Jesus Christ. Recall to yourself a glimpse of Jesus – teaching, healing, dying on the first Good Friday, rising at the first Easter. That is the likeness of the invisible God.

Normally we read as quickly as possible, because we are reading newspapers, light fiction, business letters, technical publications or textbooks. Or when we are studying a subject, we read as critically as possible. For a change, try reading suitable parts of the Bible as lovingly as possible – lingering over the scene, noticing every detail as if you had been there, asking what it shows you of God. Such 'meditation' on the Bible supplies a solid basis for prayer – and life.

When you have got clearer in your mind the reality of God, coming to you in Jesus, stepping out of the pages of the Bible, you will find it easier to put together the jigsaw puzzle of your life. You will want to admit what a muddle your life has been. The pattern of your life can't be seen from the bits – unless someone has caught sight of the picture now broken up into those bits. But even more than that you will want to give thanks for the pattern which is there all the time. The advice to 'count your blessings' is an old recipe for a glad heart, because when bit by bit you lay before God what's right in your life (and in the world's) you will find that what's wrong is reduced to its proper proportions. Most of us have a natural tendency to concentrate on what's wrong – on the problems and grumbles. Prayer is vital if we are to lift up our hearts to the goodness that, as a matter of fact, surrounds us.

It is like looking out of the window on a summer's day. And this sunshine is available to us at any time, in any place, as the air is cloudless soon after the plane has left the airport.

It may help to remember ACT: Adoration, Confession, Thanksgiving. Then – if you have any time left – remember your needs. But do so before God, which makes it different from a supermarket. Jesus encouraged his followers to be thoroughly natural when talking to their Father. Anything that a Christian can rightly want, he can rightly pray for. But there are some practical points to bear in mind.

1. The words which end many prayers in church, 'through Jesus Christ our Lord', are not just a signal to the congregation to add *Amen* (which means 'We agree! So be it!'). They are words reminding us that Christian prayer is prayer which reflects the teaching and character of Jesus Christ. (If we mutter 'Grant that my enemy may slip on a banana skin', that is not prayer through Jesus Christ.) These words also remind us that Jesus Christ is the only human being who has ever been thoroughly satisfactory in God's eyes. So Christian prayer is prayer which says to God: 'I know I am human – but so is Jesus Christ! And what I ask is to be made like him!'

2. All that we need to ask for ourselves or for anyone else is that God's will may be done. We should never attempt to dictate to God.

3. Often what we need most is guidance about what God's will is. We can get this guidance by listening. But it is easy to imagine that some wish of our own has been inspired by God. It is necessary to test what we think is guidance by comparing it with the character and teachings of Jesus Christ as recorded in the Bible.

4. We rightly pray for our physical needs, not for luxuries. We ask God for daily bread, not hourly cake.

5. We state needs which God knows already, just as a human parent knows that the children need food (plus love and some fun). Why, then, ask? For the same reason that it is our duty and our pleasure to use the word 'please' at table. Probably the same food will arrive anyway, but things go better with some courtesy.

6. God normally answers our needs through the natural processes of the world he has provided, and that means that we must do our share in co-operating with him. It is no use praying for the weeds to disappear if we will not get our hands dirty. It is no use praying for distinction in an exam if we refuse to work.

7. God is free to say 'No'. That can be the best kind of answer to prayer – as we may learn after a time.

Anything that we can rightly want for ourselves, we shall naturally want for our friends; and anything we want for our friends we can mention to God. Praying for our families and friends is one of the best possible expressions of our love for them. It simply means remembering them and their needs before God. While the whole point of prayer is that God's will (not ours or theirs) may be done, you will find that when you have prayed for people you will have a more loving attitude to them as you meet them. Your prayer has not only shown your care – it has deepened it.

Anything we want for our friends we want for those who have a claim on our active sympathy because they have to face suffering – either in the body or in the mind. So we remember before God people who are sick in hospital or at home, people who undergo the bitter experiences of loneliness and despair, and people whose lives have been devastated by violence or some other disaster. This prayer for God's world puts the world where it belongs – in God's hands. But you will find that just as prayer for your friends deepens your friendship, so prayer or 'intercession' for the world strengthens your caring about it.

After praying, you will want to find out whether you can help anyone who is sick or lonely, and how you can fight poverty and war. You will feel more responsible, more involved, more eager.

After being involved in other people's problems, or in trying to do something about the world's giant problems, you are likely to feel tired and depressed – for the problems are complicated, people can be awkward, the tragedies of the world can be completely overwhelming. Then you will want to go back to God in prayer, leaving the problems with him for a time before you begin your own work again. You will find that you need to be told again and again by your Father that you are not to feel responsible for everything. God alone carries the whole burden of what goes wrong – and you can watch him doing it on the cross. And then you will find that you can take up your duties again refreshed, co-operating with God.

Prayer changes us

Is it necessary to do all these things in order to be any good at prayer? No! These points are merely suggestions which others have found useful. They are not meant to make you feel guilty. It is for you to find your own way of praying. One of the wisest things ever said about prayer was this: 'Pray as you can, don't pray as you can't.' But it helps to remember also that what is our way of praying at one stage in our lives may not be so satisfactory at the next stage. Our circumstances change, our personalities develop – and so should our prayers. For no one can say before death that he or she has reached the end of the road of prayer. When it comes to praying, we are all beginners.

Is it necessary to kneel when praying? No! Kneeling is a traditional gesture of respect, but you can pray sitting or standing – millions of Christians have done so. Find out what bodily position helps you most. Almost everyone finds it easier to pray with eyes shut, but even this is not essential. You may find it helpful to begin your prayer by taking some deep breaths. They help us to relax and to remember that our prayer is not only, and chiefly, work which we do. It can be hard work, but it can also be inspired, made deep down in us by God as Spirit.

Is it the big thing to 'say your prayers' every morning and every night? No! Remembering God before you begin the day's work, and again before you sleep, clears the mind as a good paste cleans the teeth. The alternative is often to begin the day in a rush and to go to sleep worrying – and both habits are extremely bad for our spiritual health. But many people under modern conditions find themselves with too many things to do in the morning to be able to meditate calmly. Last thing at night, they are tired out. Quiet listening is far more important than 'saying your prayers' like a catalogue, and the most practical method may be to set aside some other time to listen to God – for example, early in the evening. It is best to do this every day. But once a week is better than once a month, and once a month is better than never.

Is prayer hypnotizing yourself? No! It often suggests things for us to do or be which are not what we should suggest if we were interested only in our comfort. And very seldom does it produce any great emotion. Often it is difficult, and persevering in it when there are so many distractions is a major test of one's character and willpower. Prayer is like tuning in the radio, trying to get rid of interference and rival programmes.

Is prayer escapism? No! It is the best way there is of getting inspiration and energy for our work – and it is the best way of sorting out our activities so that the peace of prayer gradually controls them all. What goes on in the time and place set aside for prayer ought to be – and can be – related very closely to what goes on in the rest of our lives. Indeed, it ought to – and can – express our lives, because it is no use praying one thing and living another. And our lives ought to – and can – express our prayer, because to work is to pray when we have first concentrated on prayer. Nowadays many people use, if not perfume, then at least a deodorant. Prayer is the perfume or deodorant of our sweaty existence.

All through the day we have opportunities to turn to God again and (as it were) shoot up 'arrow' prayers. You can pray on a bus, in a kitchen, by a machine, at a desk. Good God! My God! Thank God! Even these phrases, usually used without any real thought of God, can be silent prayers. So can the name Jesus. The Christians of Russia (and elsewhere) have for many centuries repeated what is called the 'Jesus Prayer': 'Lord Jesus Christ, Son of God, have mercy on me a sinner.' We are naturally keen on breaks for tea or coffee – but these breaks to recall or 'recollect' the presence of God are at least as refreshing.

Prayer does not change God. Indeed, the whole point of prayer is to remember that God never changes in his attitude to us and to the world. God's attitude is constantly, faithfully, the attitude of love, and it produces a definite plan for us. This plan offers guidance to us – and strength to act accordingly. In obeying that plan lies our hope; in God's will is our peace. Sometimes obedience takes all the courage we have – and more. That 'more' we get through prayer. In the garden of Gethsemane, when Jesus knelt and sweated in an agony, he asked God that he might be spared the crucifixion. 'Abba, Father, all things are possible to you; take this cup away from me.' But his natural feelings were controlled and calmed by the prayer: 'Your will be done!' And he went to the cross.

Prayer does not change God. Prayer changes us.

CHAPTER ELEVEN

We belong to the Church

We need it . . .

There is no such person as a solo Christian. We need groups to make most kinds of music – and families to grow up in – and meetings, movements and political parties to spread opinions – and organizations ranging from a farm to a nation to feed, dress, house, educate, heal, defend and entertain us. And to be Christians, we have to get together.

Perhaps the easiest way of saying what the Church really means is to say this: it is the group which helps us to listen to God. The last chapter discussed prayer as a conversation between God and you-by-yourself. And it was important to discuss prayer like that, because Christianity does offer you the immense privilege and happiness of being able to talk confidently and intimately with God your Father. So you are missing a highly enjoyable and strengthening experience if you never let yourself be alone with him. But many of us find that it is difficult to be alone with God for very long. It isn't only that we are so busy. Another and better reason is that we find prayer easier in a group. Young people sometimes sit cross-legged on the floor in a circle, for a time of quiet which may be all that happens – or which may lead into a few quiet things being said by members of the group. Believe it or not, that is the Church! Families can pray together (and there is a wise saying that 'the family which prays together stays together'). That can help parents to remember that they are trying to reproduce the atmosphere of a home which made it natural for Jesus of Nazereth to think of God as 'Father'. They may not be as obedient to the will of God as Mary was – but they can try. And by continuing this ancient practice of family prayers they can give their children memories which will last longer than any toy. A prayer can also be included when colleagues in a workplace come together as Christians, asking for a blessing on the work and the friendship. Neighbours can come together too, to study the Bible, to talk things over, or simply to pray. In the Bible it is promised that Jesus will be present whenever two or three are gathered together in his name, and many groups have known in their experience that this promise has been kept.

But a danger confronts any group which meets in private. It may become inward-looking, absorbed in its own group-life. It may become resentful when others try to join it – if they know when it meets and how to join. Experience shows how necessary it is to have a meeting that is public and regular, in addition to any private groups there may be. And to be practical, in a climate such as Britain's that usually means meeting in a public building.

It is often said: 'You can be a good Christian without going to church.' That is true in two ways. People who aren't regular churchgoers often have attitudes, and do actions, which are approved in the teaching of Jesus. It is also true that people heavily involved in church life have often exaggerated the importance of church buildings, church services, church organizations and church pronouncements. The State, not the Church, nowadays runs most schools, welfare services and entertainments. Much of the charitable work that is done in our society is not organized by the Church. Television has more influence than preaching. In modern life, the role of the Church has been cut down.

But that is not to say that it would be desirable to abolish the Church altogether. For what do we mean by 'the Church'? The Church does not consist of church buildings. In the New Testament the Church flourished – and did not possess a single building. The Church does not consist of ceremonies or doctrines as if it were a theatre or a lecture-hall. The Church is people! And the Church does not consist of its leaders. Over 99 per cent of the Church consists of lay people. The Church is those Christians who in a particular time and place are willing to stand up and be counted. The end of the Church would mean the end of that.

So far from deserving to be abolished, the Church as God's

people deserves to be strengthened – with muscle, not fat. For the Church is the Christian idea in a body, at work in a world which has always been full of other ideas.

It is not good enough to be in favour of Christianity as one supports a football team from an armchair in front of a TV set. Football is kept going because some people play football. Christianity has survived because of the Church and in spite of the many failures of the Church. If you doubt that, ask whether you could have become a Christian yourself had the Church never existed. Most people are attracted to Christianity by the personal example of other Christians – parents, teachers, friends, Christians met in daily life, or Christians known about from the present or the past. But that means that most Christians become Christians because they meet the people who are the Church.

Sometimes people who read the Bible are converted to Christianity just by that, but we still have to ask: who wrote the Bible, who divided it into chapters and gave it titles, who arranged for it to be a book available to that person, who could discuss with that person the full meaning of the Bible? Sometimes people who listen to the radio or watch TV are converted by that, but we have to ask: did the people who made the radio or TV programme rely entirely on other programmes for all their own knowledge of Christianity? Sometimes people have a sudden conviction that Christianity is essentially true close up – perhaps when they are walking alone. But we have to ask: how did they know what Christianity is? Sometimes people have a vision of Christ. But we have to ask: how did they recognize him? And our questions drive us back to the fact that in the plan of God Christians are made by each other, as fire is spread.

The spreading of the good news of Jesus Christ is called 'evangelism'; the word comes from the Greek for 'good news'. We are ourselves Christians because other people have been evangelists to us. But we do not really believe that it is good news if we make no effort to spread it to others. If we sincerely accept it, then we find ourselves challenged to be evangelists.

To whom are we sent as evangelists? Obviously, first to those nearest to us – the people who are within reach of our patience and affection, our encouragement and our practical help, which can show that being a Christian has improved me and which may suggest something which applies to others even though I don't 'preach'. But if we believe that Christianity means good news to ourselves and to our neighbours, we shall hope that it may be taken everywhere. And so we believe in the 'Catholic' Church, for the word 'atholic' comes from the Greek meaning 'the whole world'. The Catholic Church is the Christian group which knows that because its news is for everyone, its mission should not be narrower than the world. Any group which intends to be less than catholic is a hole-in-the-corner affair.

There are plenty of critics who delight in pointing out what is wrong and weak in the Church. But you have to ask yourself how you are linked to the lifetime of Jesus of Nazareth (about the year 30: no one knows the exact dates of the birth and death of Jesus). You have to picture the line of men and women across the centuries reaching you. Some were executed because they were Christians such as Andrew, now patron saint of Scotland, and George, now patron saint of England. Others faced great journeys and dangers in order to spread their faith in frightening places – such as Scotland and England. Others met unpopularity and had to overcome many obstacles. Others struggled with many doubts and disappointments. But all these kept the faith and passed it on so that it might be yours. And when Christians refer to the 'communion of saints', they mean fellowship with these people and millions like them – a fellowship stronger than death.

Or picture the Christians around the globe today. Christianity is more fully world-wide than any other religion has ever been, and the Church is the most international body in existence with a large membership. As the twenty-first century begins, about a third of humanity is Christian in some sense, and the number of Christians increased three-fold between 1900 and 2000.

Some Christians are richer than you. Others are much poorer. Some are very powerful. Others have to live under attacks from their government, or from prejudiced neighbours, and may be martyred. Some are honoured thinkers. Others have to be Christians in countries where most of the public references to Christianity consist of hostile propaganda. Some live in countries which have been 'Christian', at least in name, for 1,500 years. Others live in continents which the first Christians did not know existed. Some meet in churches which are among the world's chief architectural treasures. Others meet in huts or in the open air, in a small village deep in the countryside, or in a slum on the edge of a great city. This is the group, family or movement to which you can belong.

All this immense company of people has shared one wish, although many other wishes have clashed with it. It is the wish expressed by an English saint, Bishop Richard of Chichester, who died in 1253, in his prayer to see Jesus more clearly, and to love him more dearly, and to follow him more nearly.

They have seen him in each other. Often Christians have received from other Christians such understanding, forgiveness, acceptance, loyalty and friendship that they have through that experience understood more deeply what Christ's love is. And often Christians have seen in other Christians such patience, modesty, self-sacrifice, perseverance, courage and heroism that they have had a firmer faith in Christ's victory. And often Christians have seen in other Christians such a willingness to serve others (usually without any kind of publicity) that they have realized afresh how the love of Christ reaches out victoriously into all the suffering of the world. And often Christians have sensed that other Christians live very close to God, so that they have felt drawn themselves into the new relationship with the Father which Christ made possible.

Probably every group of Christians includes members who are struggling rather than winning in the achievement of this quality of life. If you are able to, help them! But there is no Christian group in the world today, or in history, which would not teach you something about Christ. And in most places where you are likely to go, you will find such a group ready to welcome you.

Unless it is shared with others, and unless it is exposed to the problems involved in living and talking with others, religion can be very selfish and very much mistaken. The remedy lies in thinking of the Church as the 'Body of Christ'. The Christian group is an instrument by which Christ continues his work in the world. It is also a body by which Christ still makes his character known. The man who first called the Church the 'Body of Christ' was Paul. He used that bold description because on the road from Jerusalem to Damascus he was overwhelmed by the conviction that to damage the Church, as he was doing, was to kick against Christ himself.

And if that is the down-to-earth truth about the Christian religion, then we have to do something practical. Just as it is not enough to play a musical instrument for our own pleasure without ever facing the challenge of joining other music-makers and facing an audience, so it is not enough to have pleasant thoughts on our own about God or about Jesus or about love – if these thoughts are not tested and strengthened by an experience shared with others.

. . . so we are baptized

The decisive step to take in joining the Body of Christ is to be baptized. And if we have never really asked ourselves what our membership of the Christian group means, the best way of deepening our understanding is to think more carefully about the meaning of Baptism. It is something more than merely pouring a little water on a baby's head, or making a converted adult take a dip in a stream. Baptism means the washing away of all that was wrong in the past. John the Baptist, the cousin and announcer of Jesus, insisted that people were sinners in need of Baptism. Jesus himself was baptized by John in the river Jordan. And the followers of Jesus used the same method to receive both Jews and Gentiles who, confessing their sinfulness, wished to become Christians.

The new Christians accepted the name of Jesus Christ and everything that went with it; they were baptized 'in the name of Jesus'. They began to share the experience which made them worship God as Three-in-One; they were baptized 'in the name of the Father and the Son and the Holy Spirit'. They joined a new people under Jesus as Lord, a people which refused to admit that any class distinctions, or barriers of any kind, had any right to spoil its fellowship. That is why Matthew's gospel ends with a picture of Jesus saying to his 'disciples' (which means pupils): 'Go to all nations and make them disciples; baptize people everywhere . . .'

In the early Christian centuries the meaning of Baptism was based on the conversion of an adult. A man or a woman accepted Jesus as Lord and Saviour, and accepted the key points of the

Church's teaching. Then he or she was immersed in the water – and it felt like death, like the death of all the evil past, like Christ's own death which offered hope for the future. Then the new Christian arose from the water, and what had seemed like burial now seemed like birth. As Paul reminded the Christians in Corinth, in his second letter: 'When anyone is united to Christ, there is a new world; the old order has gone, and a new order has already begun' (5:17).

That is still the meaning of Baptism for adults who become Christians, as hundreds of millions have over the last hundred years. Any parish priest or chaplain is always delighted to welcome candidates for adult Baptism. But at least since about AD 200 (probably since the time described in the New Testament – but the evidence is not certain), babies born in Christian families have been baptized. The Christians who are called 'Baptists' disagree with this policy, but Anglicans, like most Christians, accept it.

The Baptism of children who cannot make statements or decisions for themselves is right when there is a reasonable likelihood that they will be brought up as Christians. In homes where the parents cannot honestly promise to encourage their children to accept Jesus Christ as their Lord, Baptism may not be appropriate. However, the very act of asking for a child's Baptism almost always indicates that the family is Christian in a sense which is real, even if it is hard to bring it into line with complete commitment or orthodoxy. Wanting a 'Christening' is nowadays not usually a mere wish to be conventional. Almost all Anglicans would hope that the priest will be friendly enough to persuade the parents to have more contact with the church, for example by attending a short course which would explain what Baptism means.

In the Baptism of children of Christian parents, faith is present – the faith of the parents and of the specially appointed Christian friends known as 'godparents' or 'sponsors'. But because the infant being baptized is helpless, this service brings out dramatically the truth that in the whole story of God's people, God's reality matters even more than man's response. Before we can do anything at all, God's people are there first. God's people invite us to enter their life, which flourished long before we were born and will continue long after our deaths. At the head of God's people is the living Christ, blessing the children and calling the disciples as he did in Palestine. And behind the call of Jesus is the initiative of God, who creates and rules and who in his great love chooses us to be his people. Any Christian can administer Baptism; in an emergency, it is not necessary to find a priest first. What matters is the new birth and the new welcome into the new family, the Church.

Whether we receive it as children or as adults, Baptism makes us members of God's people. We are now (so to speak) recruits in Christ's army and limbs of Christ's body. What, then, is Confirmation?

In a tradition inherited from the Middle Ages, the service of Confirmation is the time when those who have already been baptized declare their acceptance of the Christian faith and life. They do so in front of the bishop, and then they are admitted by him into the full privileges of membership. 'Confirmation' comes from the Latin for 'strengthening', and in this service the bishop prays that these Christians may be strengthened with the gifts of the Holy Spirit, as promised to God's people. Then the bishop, representing the whole Church, lays his hands on each candidate. It is the ancient sign of blessing, often repeated in the Bible, particularly in the Acts of the Apostles when Peter and John pray that some Samaritans who have been baptized may 'receive the Holy Spirit' (8:14–17). And using words taken from the Old Testament, the bishop prays that the Holy Spirit may 'rest upon' the candidates,

the Spirit of wisdom and understanding;
the Spirit of counsel and inward strength;
the Spirit of knowledge and true godliness.

Any parish priest is glad to prepare a candidate for Confirmation. The Church has no rule about the right age. The best guidance is that a 'candidate' ought to seek Confirmation as soon as he or she has real, personal understanding of what it means to belong to the Christian group – to the Body of Christ. You need not understand much! Even the greatest Christians have understood only a little.

CHAPTER TWELVE

We inherit history

The Bible's great story

Some families have kept letters written by members of those families half a century or more ago. One of these letters may describe being in the front line in a war, or using a new invention for the first time. Letters of this sort make history come vividly alive. And it is entirely proper for you to think of the Bible as a collection of letters and other documents belonging to your family, for if you are a member of the Church you belong to the family that wrote the Bible.

You are cheating yourself if you don't make yourself at home in the Bible, and if you deny yourself the instruction and encouragement which it alone can give. Regular study of the Bible is a very important way in which the whole Church listens to God, and it is best if you can manage your own reading of the Bible every day, perhaps with the help of the notes provided by the Bible Reading Fellowship or the Scripture Union. But since you live in a world which is very different from the world when the Bible was written, you naturally ask: what authority does the Bible have over you?

If you try to reconstruct the history which lies behind the accounts given in the Bible, it is essential to use the results of modern scholarly investigations. When trying to think out what it means for your life today, it is essential to use your intelligence, after praying to God for the promised gift of guidance. What is called 'fundamentalism' – that is, the belief that the Bible contains no errors, a belief regarded by some as fundamental to Christianity – is plainly untrue. You can see this by looking at the

Bible's first two chapters. They are stories about the creation of the world, but they are not accurate science. And they are two different stories, which took this shape in different periods (contrast Genesis 1:11–13 with 2:4–6, for example). The authority of the Bible is the weight of the experience of the people who wrote it, and of the people about whom they wrote. For they experienced the activity of God in events which changed the course of history. They had the insight to see what those events meant, and they had the skill to write about it. What is true – what is the most important truth in the world – what is true not just for your information but for your life and your death – is the message given through the Bible as a result of the experiences behind the Bible. For in that message the true God is proclaimed. That is why we read in the second letter to Timothy (3:16) true words originally written in praise of the Old Testament: 'All inspired scripture has its use for teaching the truth and correcting error, or for the improvement of morals and discipline in the right way of living.'

The Bible begins with many stories told about periods before accurate history was recorded. One of them is about how Abraham left home and the rich life he had known by the river Euphrates, and in his wanderings through Palestine and the surrounding desert he experienced God in a new way. The God of Abraham became the God of his son Isaac and his grandson Jacob. And to this day, he is the God of Jews and Christians, and of Muslims too. Hundreds of years later the descendants of Abraham were in Egypt, but they left that rich civilization by the river Nile and began their wanderings again – this time under Moses. The religion they formed in that new period in the desert, before they entered Palestine, inspired much of the Old Testament and still has great influence today – for example, through the Ten Commandments. The commandments show that Israel's religion was meant to be as clean as the desert itself. God's people were to worship him alone – not sacrificing to the gods who represented sex, power and good harvests; not bowing down to gods who were no more than carved statues; not using God's name lightly. Every seven days, a whole day was to be set aside for rest and worship. And God's people were to treat each other with dignity. Fathers and mothers were to be honoured. There was to be no murder or theft. There were to be no false accusations. Each man's wife, family and property were to be respected as his, within the fellowship of God's people.

When Jesus came, he summed up the commandments in two, both quoted from other parts of the Old Testament. God must be loved with the whole personality. One's neighbours must be loved as one loves oneself – and as we have seen, by 'neighbour' Jesus meant every other human being. But before that understanding could be reached, much had to happen. For one thing, the Jewish nation had to lose its political independence.

About a thousand years before Christ, Saul, the first King of the Jews, was replaced by the more attractive and successful David – and David was succeeded by his son Solomon. It was David who made Jerusalem the capital. It was Solomon who built the temple in Jerusalem. But the ideal of wise government and glorious worship did not last. First the northern kingdom of the Jews, around Samaria, fell to the Assyrian invaders. Then Jerusalem fell to the empire of Babylon. However, during the quarrels, corruptions and tragedies of these years a highly impressive line of men, the prophets, arose. Amos, one of the first of the great prophets, was a shepherd demanding justice in society rather than sacrifices in the temple. Jeremiah preached with a rare courage against the nationalism of his own people in Jerusalem.

When some of the Jews were allowed to return to Jerusalem, their return was celebrated in the sublime poetry which we can read in chapters 40–55 of the book of Isaiah. Although disappointments and disasters followed their return to Jerusalem, and some of the Jews naturally grew narrow and bitter, this poetry has never been forgotten as a call to courage and hope. It was in this period that the Old Testament was put together. 'Testament' means 'covenant' or 'agreement'. The Old Testament expressed the faith that God had made an agreement with Abraham and his descendants, for ever. The Ten Commandments and the other laws associated with Moses attempted to state what God demanded as his side of the bargain, and the prophets frequently denounced Israel for failing to live up to the agreement. But the prophets taught that God was patient and loyal, and Jeremiah (for one) looked forward to a new covenant: 'This is the covenant . . . says the Lord, I will set my law within them and write it on their hearts; I will become their God and they shall become my people' (31:1–33).

Basically, that is the promise with which the Old Testament ends. The promise does not come true in the events covered by the Old Testament. Nor does the answer come in the books called the Apocrypha, which in many Bibles are printed between the Old and the New Testaments. These are books of varying value. They formed part of the Old Testament in Greek for the Jews now scattered in many places, but they were not acknowledged by the Jews in Palestine as having the same authority as the main books of the law, the prophets and the histories.

But the answer came. A new agreement was made between God and us. A new age began.

The life of Jesus cannot be understood unless we remember that the Old Testament was what he was taught in the school at Nazareth, and the Old Testament was what he could quote – to himself when asking himself in the desert what his work was going to be, and to others when his work became the preaching (by word and deed) of the good news of God's rule. For example, Jesus referred to himself as the 'Son of Man', an expression then commonly used. To understand the reference, you have to turn to the seventh chapter of the Book of Daniel, where there is a dream of the 'Son of Man' going in glory to God. There, the 'Son of Man' is a man who represents God's people.

Jesus never wrote a book. He lived a life, and he founded a new community, God's new people. But some of the letters written by Paul have survived, to give us authentic and unforgettable pictures of the living faith of the Church in its early years. So have a few other documents – for example, John the Divine's vision of the complete triumph of Jesus, written in a Roman prison on the island of Patmos: 'Then I saw a new heaven and a new earth . . . I saw the holy city, new Jerusalem, coming down out of heaven from God, made ready like a bride adorned for her husband' (21:1, 2). And four gospels have been treasured by the Christians from the first century AD onwards.

The oldest and shortest of these gospels is by Mark, said by tradition to have been a personal assistant both to Paul and Peter. He probably wrote it in Rome soon after the execution of those two great leaders, to strengthen his fellow-Christians for martyrdom (a word which means 'witness', for these Christians regarded their deaths as acts of witness to the living Christ). Matthew's gospel presents Jesus as the new Moses and includes the Sermon on the Mount. Luke (a doctor) portrays Jesus as the healer and friend, and gives us most of the famous parables; and this gospel is followed by a second volume, the Acts of the Apostles, showing how the message and work of Jesus spread from Jerusalem to Rome. John's gospel goes deeper than the others and is the fruit of long experience. It is a drama, like a film with a message, rather than a detailed reconstruction of what happened. It shows that the glory of Jesus is revealed in 'signs' – in particular, the sign of the cross. It shows what the coming of Jesus means, as the light of the world, and in particular it shows the intimate union between Jesus and his disciples who become his friends.

Gradually the Christians agreed that the four gospels, with Paul's letters and some other documents, were so valuable that they must be put alongside the Old Testament, as the Christian 'scriptures' (or writings). When the Roman Empire did its utmost to stamp out Christianity, the persecutors tried to get hold of these scriptures and destroy them. Any Christians who handed the books over were called *traditores*; from that word comes our 'traitors'.

God's people existed before these books were written. The stories of Abraham, Moses and the kings of Israel were told around camp fires before they were told in books. The story of Jesus was told in Christian sermons before it was told in the gospels. But these books, when written, were rightly honoured, because with a tremendous power they told of the events which had created God's people. Their authority for God's people was now unique. And although many hundreds of thousands of books have been written in the course of time, discussing the significance of the events recorded in the Bible, no book has ever been given the authority which the Bible will now always have.

Preaching to the Athenians and writing to the Romans, Paul taught that God had to a certain extent revealed himself to people who were neither Jews nor Christians. In our time, when it is easier than ever before for Christians to understand and appreciate other religious traditions, there is more agreement than ever to respect much that is good and true in the scriptures of the Muslims, Hindus, Buddhists and others. There is only one God, and it is clear that he is called by many names and worshipped according to many traditions. But it remains true that nowhere in the history of the world have there been events with results similar to the results of the events recorded in the Bible; and nowhere in the literature of the world is there a library like the Christians' Bible.

Millions of people remain loyal Jews despite many persecutions, the worst of which were inflicted by people calling themselves Christians. Inevitably Jews do not place the books of the New Testament on the same level as those of the Old – although many Jews are prepared to recognize Jesus as a great Jewish prophet and to forgive Christians for their cruelties. It is right for Christians to admit that they have lost much by getting out of touch with Jews, and that they have often behaved towards Jews in a way which is plainly condemned by Jesus. But it is also right for Christians to make their great claims about him. For Jesus summed up all that was best in the Old Testament, while getting rid of the national pride and the insistence on strict obedience to detailed religious laws. Jesus showed that all men and women, including the strictest Jews, were sinners – and Jesus offered all a new start. It was in truth a new covenant, written on the hearts of all who responded to the challenge and appeal of Jesus. As the centuries passed, the number of Christians grew into millions. Amazingly, the Christian Church proved stronger than the Roman Empire which tried to suppress it. The more it was made to suffer, the stronger the Church grew; the blood of martyrs was the seed of the Church.

The Bible reaches Britain

From one not very important part of the Roman Empire, Judaea, the Christian faith was carried as far as another, Britain – where the first and most famous martyr was Alban, put to death in 305 (or thereabouts). Within 300 years of the death of Jesus, a Christian (Constantine) was Emperor of Rome. When the Empire was overwhelmed by the surrounding barbarians, the Church remained standing – the guardian not only of the Christian faith but also of civilization, knowledge, gentleness, law and order.

Only in some provinces such as Britain did the Church disappear as an organization. And in these dark ages the work of the Christian missionaries survived and flourished in Cornwall, Wales, Ireland and the lowlands of Scotland, inspired by saints such as David (in Wales), Patrick (in Ireland), Ninian and Columba (in Scotland).

It was because the Church played such a vitally important role in European history after the fall of the Roman Empire that it became so powerful – so deeply respected, and so wealthy. In Rome the Popes became world-leaders, much as the Emperors had been. The first great Pope, Gregory, saw it as his mission to conquer new lands for Christianity. With great boldness he sent Augustine from Rome to England in 597, as the first Archbishop of Canterbury; and Ethelbert, King of Kent, was soon converted.

Slowly England became part of the Catholic Church. In the North the most heroic missionaries – men such as Cuthbert who lies buried in Durham Cathedral, or Chad the first Bishop of Lichfield – looked for inspiration not to Canterbury but to the holy islands of Iona (off Scotland) and Lindisfarne (off Northumberland). But gradually all the English Christians were brought together into one Church under the Pope and the Archbishops of Canterbury and York. In fact the English Church was one while the country was still divided into tribal kingdoms. It became famous for its scholars such as Bede in Jarrow, and for its Christian kings such as Alfred the Great, King of Wessex, and Edward the Confessor, who founded Westminster Abbey. In its turn England produced missionaries such as Boniface, the man from Devon who led the chief Christian mission in Germany.

The Norman conquest of England in 1066 linked England more firmly with the rest of Europe, and the Norman churches which still survive are reminders of the strength and discipline brought by the invaders. But the Church became in many ways a champion of freedom. Archbishop Anselm, a famous philosopher, stood up to William the Conqueror's son. Thomas Becket resisted Henry II and was murdered by Henry's knights in Canterbury Cathedral (1170). Another Archbishop of Canterbury, Stephen Langton, was at the head of the barons who forced King John to accept the English liberties set forth in the Magna Carta (1215).

More important than politics was the growth in mind and spirit in the Middle Ages. Schools, universities and hospitals were founded. The monks, giving themselves to the worship of God, were in many cases also good farmers or scholars. The friars – monks not confined to a monastery – took the love of Christ to the poor of the towns, following the examples of St Francis in Italy and St Dominic in Spain and France. Some saintly bishops such as Hugh of Lincoln inspired the parishes. On pilgrimage to the tomb of Thomas Becket, a pageant of humanity in the fourteenth century passes through the pages of Geoffrey Chaucer's *Canterbury Tales*, and noble writings have been left by more spiritually minded Christians such as Lady Julian of Norwich. Some purity was lost when the Church became so closely identified with a whole society. (For example, the Church now permitted 'just' wars although the early Christians had been pacifists, rejecting everything to do with war.) But there were many gains.

The Christian civilization of the Middle Ages was broken up by many changes in the sixteenth century, the age of Reformation. Today it seems a vanished world. But you can feel its beauty and its faith near you if you go into an old cathedral or parish church, or if you listen to an old carol or to the sound of church bells. You can then know for yourself that some rich and astonishing chapters in the story of God's people were written when the Bible had been completed. Today, all this is your heritage.

CHAPTER THIRTEEN

We are Anglicans

How it began

The Christian Church is tragically divided. It ought to be possible just to say, 'We are Christians.' But the fact is that in order to be a full Christian you have to gather regularly with your fellow-Christians, and in order to do this you have to belong to one of the churches into which the Christian Church is now split.

The 'ecumenical' (from the Greek for 'world-wide') movement for Christian unity has developed since about 1910 and has already made great advances. The relationships between the divided churches have been transformed. In many practical ways they co-operate, and over more and more theological problems they agree. There is no good reason why our present divisions should continue for much longer. On the contrary, it is widely agreed that the need is great for reunion between the churches – a union of the kind that Christ commands, the way he wishes us to follow. What is that way? This urgent question cannot be answered unless we pray for guidance, and unless we take trouble to meet members of other churches. If we are to unite with each other, we must love each other; and if we are to love each other, we must meet.

Anglicans belong to the World Council of Churches, formed in 1948, and take part in the life and work of 'Christians together' in the local council of churches. Since the 1960s many strong links of understanding and friendship have been formed with the Roman Catholic Church, and there have been negotiations for full reunion with Methodists, Presbyterians and others. (Methodism was founded by an Anglican, John Wesley, who died in 1791. Presbyterians believe that the 'presbyter' should be the senior officer in the local church, but do not have bishops.) Closer relationships involving 'mutual recognition' (as when friends meet) have been established with Protestants in Germany and Scandinavia. Anglicans already belong to some United Churches overseas – but not yet in Britain.

Anglicans have no right to condemn any other church. Instead, they gladly acknowledge that God has blessed and used their fellow-Christians in many ways. All that Anglicans need to say is that while the Christian churches still pray and work for reunion it is right for them to be proud of this special heritage. The Anglican tradition preserves the essential beliefs which are held in common by all Christians. It also contains many treasures which should be contributed to the wider Church in the fuller unity which must come.

The word 'Anglican' comes from the Latin for 'English', because the pattern of life in the modern, world-wide Anglican Communion was set by the changes made in the Church of England during the Protestant Reformation of the sixteenth century. These were great changes, made possible by the rejection of the claims of the Popes at the time.

The Bible and the church services were translated from Latin into English so that all could understand. Christian faith and Christian life became simpler and were freed from control by the priest. But the churches inherited from the Middle Ages were still used, and there was much continuity in what went on inside them. The Church of England emerged from the Reformation both Protestant and Catholic in spirit, although its conservatism was criticized by many other Protestants and its refusal to obey the Pope was regarded as heretical by many other Catholics.

Some of the reasons for these changes were political. Henry VIII sought from the Pope a decision that his marriage with Catherine of Aragon had not been a true marriage. And in Rome the Pope refused. The King's reply was that no foreigner such as the Pope must be allowed any authority in England. Between 1532 and 1534 seven Acts of Parliament separated the Church of England from Rome – and made the King himself its 'supreme head' on earth. But it was not simply a question of a lustful (and repulsive) monarch wanting a divorce. Actually, what he wanted was a decree of 'nullity' to say that his marriage with Catherine had been no marriage at all, for she had first been the wife of his dead brother, Arthur – and, quoting the book of Leviticus in the Bible which prohibited marriage with a dead brother's wife, Henry persuaded himself that Catherine's failure to produce a son was a sign of God's wrath. What really mattered was that Henry needed a son and heir; it was dangerous to leave the crown of England to a woman.

Curiously, it was under a queen, Elizabeth I, that the Church of England achieved a settlement which proved lasting apart from some twenty years in the middle of the seventeenth century. In 1649 Oliver Cromwell and other extreme Protestants or 'Puritans' succeeded in overthrowing and executing Charles I, one of the charges against the King being his loyalty to the Anglican way of running the Church. But the Puritan revolution was not permanent. The Church of England was established once more as the National Church in 1660, and when James II, who had been converted to Roman Catholicism, tried to alter this, it was the King who found himself in exile (in 1688). The Church of England prevailed against Oliver Cromwell and James II because this National Church had firmly taken root in the English soil. It had been 'established' by the State, but more important, it was accepted by many of the people, partly out of patriotism.

When England became the centre of a vast empire over the next 250 years, naturally the English took the customs of their National Church wherever they went. So Anglicanism was built up in the United States and Canada, in India and Africa, in Australia and New Zealand, and in many other places around the world.

But to say that the Church of England's history cannot be separated from the history of England, or that the missionary expansion of Anglicanism accompanied the expansion of the British Empire, merely tells us something about the past. It does not answer the question whether Anglicanism has the right to survive now when England itself is a very different country. In the life of the world-wide Anglican Communion English domination has been rejected. There are, for example, flourishing Anglican churches in Scotland, Wales and Ireland. The Anglican or 'Episcopal' Church in the United States is important not only to its own great nation but also to the whole of Anglicanism. The Anglican churches in Africa are growing fast. Names can tell their own stories and 'Episcopal' can be used as an alternative to the English-sounding 'Anglican' because these churches are led by bishops, *episkopoi* in Greek. Or the name can be simply 'the Church of the Province of . . .' because the Anglicans or Episcopalions are united in a 'province' which is self-governing.

It seems right to say the Church of England and other churches in the world-wide Anglican Communion have shown – as the great Orthodox churches of Russia, Greece and other countries have also shown – that it is possible to remain full members of the Catholic Church without acknowledging the claims made by the Popes during and since the Middle Ages (that is, since about AD 1000). These disagreements can be explained and defended by arguments, but it would not be right to make this short book longer by criticizing fellow-Christians.

To be positive, we can rightly claim that Anglicanism has proved its spiritual value although it has been far from perfect. That can be shown by the great poets to whom the Church of England has been a home – among them William Shakespeare, John Donne, George Herbert, William Cowper, William Wordsworth, S. T. Coleridge, John Keble, Alfred Tennyson, Matthew Arnold, Christina Rossetti, T. S. Eliot, W. H. Auden. Such poets would not have loved the Church of England if it was nothing more than the cold institution described by its critics. They have found something alive, authentic and good in the life of their English church – its beautiful services, its constant emphasis on the Bible, its tolerance, its respect for the views and interests of the many rather than the few, its stability despite the freedom and variety in its life.

Worship and doctrine

Anglican worship has been 'corporate' or 'common' (all together) but dignified. Thomas Cranmer, then Archbishop of Canterbury, edited the Book of Common Prayer – one of the noblest books in the English language, able to speak to the heart but almost all the time maintaining the highest standards of beauty. It was issued in 1549, but changes were made in 1552, 1559, 1604 and 1662.

Another very influential Anglican prayer book was issued for Scotland in 1637. This was unpopular among most of the Scots, but something unexpected happened later. When the United States had won their independence, it was in Scotland that the first Anglican bishop for America was consecrated (in 1784) – and so the Scottish prayer book influenced the first American prayer book (in 1789).

In recent years almost all the Anglican churches in the world have issued more modern services, since the language of 1549 or 1637 is no longer always understood. Many of these services have allowed greater freedom than Cranmer thought proper, so that contemporary concerns and hopes can be voiced. Another great enrichment has come through the increasing use of hymns – some of them now old and very famous, but some new and experimental. There has also been the development of music for the choir and the organ. A great musical tradition has grown up since the Book of Common Prayer was first printed, and every century including our own has added to it. The music in some Anglican cathedrals and college chapels is world-renowned, and the Royal School of Church Music unites many thousands of parish church choirs in aiming at the best. But across the centuries the backbone of Anglican worship has remained 'liturgical', involving the use of words known to all, as a way of offering the prayer of all. ('Liturgy' comes from a Greek word meaning a job done for the public's benefit.)

This worship is dominated by the Bible. For hundreds of years churchgoers loved to hear the magnificent English of the Psalms (the Old Testament's hymns) as translated by Bishop Miles Coverdale in 1535 – and the lessons from the Authorized Version of the Bible issued in 1611 during Shakespeare's lifetime. Then modern translations became necessary. and they are being used in more and more churches. Still, however, the principle remains: our common prayer is best when together we have heard the Word of God through the 'Scriptures'. Anglicans sit under the Bible.

Anglican 'doctrine' or teaching is therefore based on the Bible. This is the Church of England's official definition, adopted in 1973:

The doctrine of the Church of England is grounded in the holy Scriptures, and in such teachings of the ancient Fathers and Councils of the Church as are agreeable to the said Scriptures. In particular such doctrine is found in the Thirty-nine Articles of Religion, the Book of Common Prayer, and the Ordinal.

The 'Articles of Religion' mentioned in that definition are a document, last revised in 1571, stating the Church of England's position in the theological controversies of the time. The Ordinal is the collection of services for 'ordaining' or setting aside the clergy.

Anglicanism accepts and devoutly uses the two sacraments founded by Jesus Christ himself. These are Baptism and Holy Communion. A sacrament has been described as 'the use of material things as signs and pledges of God's grace, and as a means by which we receive his gifts'. Thus the use of water in Baptism is a sign of God's saving goodness, and a means of receiving it. The use of bread and wine in Holy Communion is a sign that Christ died for us, and it is a means of sharing his 'risen' life.

Anglicanism also accepts and devoutly repeats the two creeds which have come down from the days before the Church was divided. One is called the 'Apostles' Creed'. It was not written by the apostles, but it began in the teaching given to candidates for Baptism in Rome and elsewhere. The word 'apostle' means 'envoy', and this creed states briefly – almost as in a headline – what was thought to be essential in the message which the apostles passed on to the Church. The other creed is called the 'Nicene Creed', from the Council of the Church held in 325 in the town of Nicaea. (Some words were added later.) It states briefly what was thought to be most important in the Church's faith – that Jesus was both truly human and truly divine. Another, longer document called the 'Athanasian Creed' is also printed in old prayer books, although nowadays it is seldom used. But the majestic hymn 'We praise thee, O God' (in Latin, *Te Deum Laudamus*), written in about 400, is often sung or said in Anglican worship. It may be regarded as a kind of creed, being a song of Christians who are joyful and triumphant.

Essentially, what Anglicans do when they use these creeds, or sing *Te Deum*, is to state that they are glad to stand in the tradition of faith which the creeds have expressed for so long.

Anglican life

Anglican life is not confined to what was laid down explicitly in the Bible or in the ancient church or in the Tudor age. It has been a living experience, changing as faithful Christians have changed. Successive generations, and very different groups and individuals, have added to the riches of Anglican worship and to the vigour of Anglican thought and life. All the clergy of the Church of England now have to agree to a declaration which states that the Church's faith is 'uniquely revealed in the holy Scriptures' and 'set forth in the Catholic creeds' but that the Church has a duty to proclaim it afresh to each generation.

In Anglicanism, lay people matter. (Here 'lay' means 'not clergy' and comes from the Greek for 'the people', *laos*.) Almost all the clergy have spent a lot of their time out and about, visiting people in their homes and trying to help people with problems. Many priests have served as chaplains in schools and colleges, in the Forces, in industry, in hospitals and prisons. The Anglican conviction is that the Church ought to be thoroughly involved in the life of the people.

Other parts of the Anglican Communion have their own ways of reaching out to the people, but in the Church of England all who live in the area known as the 'parish' are regarded as this Church's responsibility. Unless they belong to another religious body, the parish church is their church. All who worship regularly in that church, and who are baptized and over sixteen, are entitled to have their names on the 'electoral roll'. Each year those on this list elect the Parochial Church Council, which co-operates with the rector or vicar in the initiation, conduct and development of church work both within the parish and outside – and which controls most of the parish church's financial and other affairs. The chief lay officers are the two churchwardens, elected annually and assisted by elected 'sidesmen' and 'sideswomen'.

At any rate since the eighteenth century, Anglican laymen and women have been encouraged to think for themselves, and have been free to do so without fear of heresy-hunts. Priests have also been encouraged to be scholars and thinkers, with the freedom needed to seek truth and express it. For example, Anglicanism has encouraged the study of the Bible by scientifically historical methods. The teachers of the Church have been men and women educated in ordinary colleges, familiar with contemporary thought, and often teaching and writing in the universities. And the Church has been heavily involved in education at almost every level. For centuries, the Church of England controlled almost all the schools in the nation. Still this Church maintains many thousands of church schools, and also colleges of higher education, within national systems. A typically Anglican prayer is that 'true religion and sound learning' may flourish together.

This involvement in the life of society has brought problems. For example, there has been the problem of the relationship of religion and politics.

For centuries the Church of England was controlled by the English Crown and Parliament, representing the lay people of England. Now that the Church has its own democratic assemblies (the Church of England has its General Synod, and also Diocesan and Deanery Synods) most people feel that these are the bodies that ought to speak up on behalf of lay Christians. So the links between Church and State in England are being altered, although the Sovereign has remained 'Supreme Governor' of the Church of England since the reign of Elizabeth I. Nowadays, the actual power of the State over the Church is limited. The General Synod can authorize new forms of worship and new expressions of the historic doctrines, and is almost entirely left by Parliament to make the rules which members of the Church ought to keep. Representatives of the Church suggest the names of new bishops. No other Anglican Church has recently been controlled by the government of its country. Anglicanism in Ireland ceased to be 'established' by the State in 1871; in Wales, in 1920.

The problem of religion and politics has led to many controversies. Most members of the Church are nervous about 'mixing religion and politics', and are particularly suspicious of priests who 'get mixed up in politics'. This is understandable. Christianity has a message which goes far deeper than any political programme could ever do, and the Church should not be identified with any political party. But there ought to be some connection between religion and politics. Religion ought to inspire us with the vision of God's love, and what God wants for everyone is a life much wider than going to church. The gospels show very clearly that Jesus was interested in human life, not only in religion; indeed, his passionate hope was that government by God over the whole of life would come into being all over the world. In particular, Jesus expressed by word and action the Father's love for people on the margins of well-fed and respectable society. Jesus not only healed and taught such people; he had meals with them, he was their friend. Countless Christians have been challenged by that example to protest against injustice and exploitation, to demand fairer laws, to break down divisions, to help the sick and unfortunate, to stand alongside the poor; and many Anglicans have been among these true followers of the Son of Man who 'came not to be served but to serve' (Mark 10:45).

In a society where many professions exist to offer social service or health care or education or other forms of service to the public, it is right that Christians should be foremost in joining those professions, even though the pay may be less than they could earn elsewhere. And in a democratic society it is both possible and necessary for Christians not only to offer quiet help to those around them, and not only to support the work of charities, but also to use their voices and their votes in order that a better society may reflect more of the vision of Jesus, all the time being down-to-earth as Jesus was.

Some famous Anglican thinkers have disturbed the complacent by preaching a vision of a society founded on justice. The greatest names in the past (in England) are those of the Victorian, F. D. Maurice, and the two twentieth-century bishops, Charles Gore (of Birmingham and Oxford) and William Temple (of Manchester, York and Canterbury). Some Anglicans have taken the lead in protests against injustices and evil. In nineteenth-century England, for example, William Wilberforce campaigned against the trade in slaves, Josephine Butler against the men who made money out of prostitutes, and Lord Shaftesbury against the use of children as labourers in factories and mines.

In the twentieth century the Church of England sponsored

studies and action in response to the problems of unemployment and poverty in its own country: for example, a careful report on conditions in the inner cities and run-down council estates had the positive title *Faith in the City* and was followed up by positive action supported by the Church Urban Fund, which gave grants to many locally planned projects for the improvement of neighbourhoods. And in other countries Anglicans have earned widespread praise – along with much criticism – for their role in campaigns for social justice. They were prominent in the victorious struggle against apartheid in South Africa and in the civil rights movement which protested against discrimination based on racial prejudice in the USA. Anglicans have defended the rights of Native peoples in Canada, of Aborigines in Australia and of Maoris in New Zealand – and have made stands in public against tyranny and corruption in the new nations of Africa. Archbishop Janani Luwum paid with his life for standing up to Idi Amin, the brutal dictator of Uganda. Of course not all Anglicans have been heroic enough, but at least they know that the best tradition of their Church is a summons to courage.

Problems of a very different sort have been raised by the work of the scholars on the Bible and on the traditions of the Church. Anglican scholars, possessing so much freedom, have often reached critical conclusions. These have often challenged the orthodoxy of less critical members of the Church. Such problems have led to fierce controversies, but in these – as in debates on political matters – the view of the Church as a whole has not been finally expressed by any leader. The mind of the Church has been made known gradually, as a result of free thought and free speech.

It is sometimes suggested that Anglicanism is a mere debating society, composed of individuals who are so 'liberal' that they agree about nothing. But Anglicanism has in it strong evangelical and strong catholic elements, reminding it that it exists in order to be obedient to Jesus Christ. The word 'liberal' ought to mean that we believe in liberty, particularly in the freedom to accept what is true in what is new: it does not necessarily commit us to any particular opinion, or to any 'ism' which is a whole system of beliefs.

In practice, whenever any change is proposed by those who may be called 'liberals', others are likely to make a challenge: is this being sufficiently loyal to the Bible and the Church's tradition? And whenever any change is resisted by those who may be called 'conservatives' others are likely to make another challenge: is this being sufficiently sensitive to the Christian duty to communicate the good news to a society as it actually exists now? The controversies that result can be painful and seriously divisive, but at least the questions are out in the open and the tensions are the results of trying to make sure that Christianity is relevant without ceasing to be Christian.

The evangelical (or 'low church') movement in Anglicanism safeguards the insistence of the Protestant Reformation on the right and the duty of each person to make his or her own decision to be reconciled to God through Jesus Christ. There is great emphasis on the fact that salvation from sin is the free gift of God, not earned by any good that we may do but given to those who in simple trust accept Jesus Christ as Saviour and Lord. With this great importance is laid on the privilege and duty of personal Bible study. Worship is simple, making clear that what matters is the response to the message in the Bible. Prayer is simple, being attention to the Father who is revealed in the Bible. From prayer the Christian arises to live in the light given by the Bible. And resulting from this, great emphasis is laid on evangelism – spreading the good news of Jesus Christ, at the centre of the Bible.

Anglican evangelicals have often been marked by enthusiasm and attractiveness in daily life, for their Bible-based religion has been warmly personal. Evangelicalism revived during the eighteenth century – at a time when much of the rest of Anglican life had grown cold because of a dull emphasis on being moderate, reasonable and respectable. In the twentieth century, the evangelical movement revived again – and now it is again meeting a spiritual need.

The catholic (or 'high church') movement in Anglicanism safeguards the continuity with the Church before the Reformation, and greatly values connections with other Christians in our own time, remembering that most Christians in the world today belong to the Roman Catholic Church or to one of the Orthodox Churches.

Anglo-Catholicism tends to have more elaborate services, and to stress the traditions of the Church. It was strong during the seventeenth century as a reaction against the Puritanism of Oliver Cromwell and the like. It revived during the nineteenth century, in what was known as the Oxford Movement, as a reaction against compromise with the materialism of modern society. It has restored much of the old beauty to churches and church services – and has restored the old insistence on personal holiness through self-discipline. The Anglican communities of monks and nuns have been examples to many. And many Anglicans have found it spiritually helpful to base their life of prayer and discipleship not on intense emotions which can come and go, but on what is given to them, the sacraments.

Whatever their differences of emphasis, all accept and honour the threefold 'ministry' of bishops, priests and deacons. 'Minister' comes from the Latin for servant, and a person who is a minister serves Christ, the Lord of the Church, and the whole Church, the whole people. The system of having bishops as leaders is known as 'episcopacy'. Bishops have been the main leaders of the Church since the second century, and in many ways they carry on the work of the apostles. A bishop is therefore a living sign of the continuity of the Church, and of its unity. He is a 'father-in-God' to the clergy and the people in the 'diocese'. He is also a teacher of the Christian and catholic faith, and a planner and inspirer of evangelism and further advance. 'Priest' is the shortened form of the word 'presbyter', or elder. Priests preside at the Holy Communion, lead local congregations, try to reach all who need their help, and assure sinners of God's forgiveness and healing. 'Deacon' is from a Greek word meaning 'servant'. In Anglicanism, the deacon is usually in training to be a priest.

Considerable numbers of women have been ordained as Anglican priests and deacons in recent years, and in some Anglican churches there are women bishops. Not all Anglicans agree with this development, and in England arrangements have been made for parishes which disagree with it to be ministered to by bishops who also disagree, but among the priests of the Church of England women provided one in ten by the end of the twentieth century.

The main argument put forward by those who disagree is that no woman is named as an apostle or 'presbyter' in the New Testament, or is found among the priests in the Catholic tradition over many centuries. The change can seem so great that some think it ought not to be made without a decision by the whole Church.

But the main argument in favour of opening the ordained ministry to women is that evidently God has given many of them the abilities which are needed in the work of bishops, priests and deacons – and many women are now convinced that they have been called by God to this work. So many Anglicans have become convinced that at a time when the full equality of women with men is widely thought to be part of the justice which God demands, the time seems right to make a change which in earlier ages seemed out of the question. What can be agreed by all Anglicans is that women are now bound to be increasingly welcome and useful in prominent roles in the Church, whether ordained or lay, whether in the local church or in a more public sphere.

Each Anglican diocese is grouped with others in a 'province'. In the British Isles, for example, there are the provinces of Canterbury and York, and other provinces known as the Church in Wales, the Church of Ireland and the Episcopal Church in Scotland (which, because it still wanted to be led by bishops, split from the National Church, the Church of Scotland, when that Church finally became Presbyterian in 1690).

Each Anglican province manages its own affairs and has its own character – a development which has been vitally important, since by the 1990s more than three-quarters of the regular membership of Anglican churches practised their religion outside England. But each is in 'communion' or full fellowship with the Church of England and in particular with the Archbishop of Canterbury, who is the 'Primate' or senior bishop of 'All England'. Once every ten years all the Anglican bishops meet in the Lambeth Conference. It is so called from Lambeth Palace, the London home of the Archbishops of Canterbury, but now it meets in Canterbury itself. Every other year, the smaller Anglican Consultative Council meets, wherever it chooses. Frequently the senior bishops keep in touch with each other, either by electronic mail or by face-to-face meetings. And although English is used widely, this international Anglican Communion now includes many millions of people who do not speak it.

The threefold ministry of bishop, priest and deacon is based on the Catholic way of ordaining them – by prayer with the 'laying on of hands' by a bishop. At the consecration of a new bishop, a minimum of three other bishops must 'lay on hands' in prayer. There is plenty of evidence that from early times the work of bishops, priests and deacons has been of great importance. And although the Reformation in the sixteenth century caused many controversies about the nature of the ordained ministry, there is plenty of evidence that those controversies are dying down nowadays. In recent years, representatives of Anglicanism have held careful talks with Roman Catholics, with the Orthodox churches which preserve the oldest living form of church life, with the Lutherans who preserve the name of Martin Luther the hero of the Protestant Reformation, and with Presbyterians and Methodists – and have joined them in publishing documents to show how much the Churches agree. Studies sponsored by the World Council of Churches have also shown a unity which is very promising.

The work of bishops, priests and deacons has been work for Christ, representing Christ. It has been part of the vitality of the catholic Church – which since the sixteenth century has (Anglicans believe) included Anglicanism. It has served the laity who are most of the Church and it has been part of the work of spreading the good news of Christ, the central message of the Bible.

CHAPTER FOURTEEN

We take part in the Holy Communion

Why we do this

Every full member of the Church ought to take part regularly in the Holy Communion if he or she can.

People sometimes ask: why go to church, when you can watch hymn-singing and discussions on TV? There are two answers. The first is that some people are in rebellion against the tyranny of TV. When they want to worship God, as they regularly do, they want to do it themselves in company with their fellow-Christians, and not leave it to the few who appear on the TV screen. When they want to hear the good news from God expounded and interpreted, they prefer listening to a preacher who is human in front of them. They enjoy the beauty and peace of the building. They enjoy singing with people they know. They enjoy meeting friends afterwards – and they may even enjoy the walk!

Perhaps such reasons for going to church may not convince you. Knowing how good some of the religious programmes are, you may prefer to stay at home watching. But there is another reason for going to church, and it is a far stronger one. No TV set has been invented which passes bread and wine round, making a Christian community.

This is the one service which Jesus Christ himself founded, at his last supper with his disciples. It has been the heart of Christian worship ever since that evening in the upper room in Jerusalem – in a modern city just as in the days when almost all Christians lived close to the land they cultivated. Through many centuries already, this has been the mystery which has gathered the followers of Jesus and kept them close to him.

Paul's first letter to the Christians in Corinth contains the earliest surviving description of the Holy Communion, in chapter 11.

> The tradition which I handed on to you came to me from the Lord himself: that the Lord Jesus, on the night of his arrest, took bread and, after giving thanks to God, broke it and said: 'This is my body, which is for you; do this as a memorial of me.' In the same way, he took the cup after supper and said: 'This cup is the new covenant sealed by my blood. Whenever you drink it, do this as a memorial of me.' For every time you eat this bread and drink the cup, you proclaim the death of the Lord, until he comes.

At that last supper before his arrest, Jesus gave thanks over the bread and wine. It was the Jewish way of saying 'grace' at a meal. When the first Christians repeated this action, it was during the course of a meal together – as Paul's letter shows. Before long the Holy Communion was made a separate service (in order to avoid problems to which Paul's letter refers), although often in our time those who have taken part in it do gather immediately afterwards for a meal or at least for a cup of coffee or tea. Here at once we see part of the meaning of this act. It is an act done by people with glad and grateful hearts. It is an act in which they enjoy some of the good things in God's creation as they eat and drink. And it is an act of fellowship.

For Christians, this is the family party. Its joy and its togetherness were indicated by Paul in the same letter. 'When we bless "the cup of blessing", is it not a means of sharing in the blood of Christ? When we break the bread, is it not a means of sharing in the body of Christ? Because there is one loaf, we, many as we are, are one body; for it is one loaf of which we all partake.' In other words, this eating and this drinking make Christians remember what they are – the Body of Christ!

It is a special kind of eating and drinking, for it is done in remembrance of Jesus. Just as the bread and the wine are taken to the 'altar' or holy table, and are taken by the priest who presides, so the life of Jesus was taken to disclose the life of God. Just as the bread is broken in order to be eaten, so the body of Jesus was broken on the cross in order to be used as the instrument of our liberation, as the placard of God's love. Just as the wine is poured out, so the blood of Jesus was shed in that great battle against evil. It is a memorial – a grateful, proud and triumphant proclamation. But it is more. When Christians eat this and drink this, they do not remember an absent friend who died long ago. They 'do this' in the conviction that their Lord is alive – and is present among them.

Through this sacrament, he is among his followers today with as much power as when he sat or stood among the apostles at the beginning. (If you are troubled by the fact that many people seem little influenced by the Holy Communion, remember how often those who saw Jesus physically failed to understand him.) Of course the bread is not his body, or the wine his blood, physically. Any chemical test would show that they haven't changed – so far as chemistry can tell. But to those who have put their trust in Jesus' promises, they have a new value, in much the same way as a piece of paper means something different to us when it has printed on it a promise to pay money. In the Holy Communion service the bread is to us Christ's body, and the wine is to us his blood. Why? Because he promised!

The priest who presides at the Holy Communion is not a magician turning one thing into another. But as he repeats the story of the last supper, as he takes, and breaks, and pours, and gives, all the Christians present are caught up into the drama – for as we 'do this' here and now we are ourselves actors in the drama, not mere spectators. And into the midst of us, sinful and blind as we are, Jesus comes. The action of eating and drinking, in this wonderfully special setting, means a 'communion' or intimate fellowship with him. In much the same way, a handshake means: I want to be your friend. Or a salute means: I obey you. Or a kiss means: I love you. We gather as friends of one another and of Jesus. We obey his order, 'Do this', as part of our whole attempt to live as he commanded.

What we celebrate

Naturally we remember the last supper and the crucifixion of Jesus. We celebrate his self-sacrifice made once and for all upon the cross. But we can only celebrate his death – we can only call that Friday 'good' – if we are convinced that he has been raised from the dead by the power and the glory of his Father and ours. Christians remember this particularly on Sunday, the first day of the week, which has replaced the Jewish Sabbath (Saturday), because on a Sunday Christians first knew that they were reunited with Jesus after his crucifixion. Every Sunday is a little Easter. As we eat and drink in fellowship with our living Lord, and in the presence of our Father, we pray that we may be filled with the Holy Spirit – so that we, too, may love. As we feed on the divine life, now among us and in us, we who believe give thanks. And now we can say in the silence of our hearts: 'Here, Lord, is my body – for you. And here is my blood – for you.' That is the living sacrifice of ourselves.

We cannot define exactly how he will keep his promise to be really present when we remember him in this supreme way, but we can share the faith expressed in the simple little poem which is attributed to Queen Elizabeth I:

> 'Twas the Word that spake it,
> He took the Bread and brake it,
> And what the Word doth make it,
> That I believe, and take it.

An act so full of meaning has to be prepared for carefully. We have come together to realize the presence of God, to whom (as the old prayer says) 'all hearts are open, all desires known'. So we pray together – as we ought already to have prayed in private – for the cleansing of our thoughts.

To help this, we are given the 'collect' or prayer which 'collects' the thoughts of the Church for this particular day or week. We are given, too, a reading from 'the epistle' – an extract from one of the letters of Paul or John. It is read to us as it was originally read to a group of Christians. Then we stand to hear an extract from one of the gospels and to join in saying the creed which is the Church's response to this cleansing revelation of God in Jesus Christ.

After the creed we pray for the Church and for the world. We remember particularly all in authority, and all who suffer in body, mind or spirit. We pray for ourselves, for our families and friends, and for the dead, that in us all God's will may be done; and we rejoice at the faithful witness of the saints in every age, praying that we may share with them in God's eternal kingdom. There are no barriers around us as we gather for this Holy Communion. We are open to the world – and to heaven.

Because we are sinners, we can say before we come to this table: 'We are not worthy so much as to gather up the crumbs.' But the bread and the wine which have been made out of the wheat and the grapes can be used to express God's creating and forgiving love; and so we offer these symbols of our own life and work – for him to make clean and useful. In this trust, we dare to join the song which, in the book of Isaiah (chapter 6), the prophet hears in the temple in Jerusalem: 'Holy, holy, holy . . .' And we dare to join in the prayer which Jesus gave to his followers: 'Our Father . . .'

Christians can turn to this feast in every conceivable variety of mood. People have taken part in the Holy Communion after being married, after being crowned, before a battle, and before dying. They have taken part in it while seated on the floor as a young people's group, while gathered around a kitchen table, while standing in a prison cell, while crowded together at a great open-air rally. We can do this before any sorrow or happiness, or before beginning a routine kind of week or day. And whatever our mood may be, we shall find that we have to adjust to the mood dictated by the Church's year – another source of variety in this endless, inexhaustible act.

In Advent when we wait for Christ's coming at Christmas, and in Lent when the days lengthen as we wait for Easter, the colour is solemn purple or blue, as we pray for the spirit of expectancy and discipline. At Christmas and Easter the colour in church is white; with great joy we recall him whose birth made us clean and whose death destroyed death's power to destroy us. At Pentecost (the English name is 'Whitsun'), when the colour is red (for fire), we recall the gift of the Holy Spirit. On the Sundays after Trinity Sunday, when the colour is green (for life), we think of the practical consequences of our belief that God has revealed his glory in the undivided splendour of the Father, the Son and the Spirit.

Whatever our own mood may be, and whatever the Church's season may be, taking part in this feast is like medicine to the sick or light to the blind. It does not matter what we call this service – 'Holy Communion', or 'the Lord's Supper', or 'the Eucharist' (from the Greek for 'Thanksgiving'), or 'the Mass' (from the Latin for 'Sent'). This supreme act of Christian fellowship makes us more deeply thankful, and sends us out into the world in the power of the Holy Spirit. Those who have shared this feast find themselves called to live and work in such a way that God is praised and seen in his glory – when these Christians are being the Body of Christ far away from any church building or service.

How often should we take part in the Holy Communion? Anglicanism leaves it to our own consciences. Some Christians who have prepared themselves carefully have found that they could not honestly do so very often – so they have not gone very often. But in Anglicanism today, more and more Christians are finding that it is best to go every Sunday to the Parish Communion. Then the Holy Communion becomes to them, all together, what it was for the first Christians and what it has been for so many millions: the Christian act of celebration. It is the Lord's own service.

CHAPTER FIFTEEN

We turn to the future

Wanting the future

The complaint is made that the Church clings to the past. If that is the whole truth about the Church, then it is a sentence of death. For to live, we must be active; to be active, we must have hope; and to have hope, we must turn to the future with zest. If the Church were to be a museum only, the stench of decay would probably be so depressing that fewer and fewer people would look into it. But that is not the whole truth!

The Christian Church has many solid reasons to be proud of its past. Jesus Christ told his followers to be like salt in the world, making history taste good, and to some extent that is what they have been. But great as the past is, the Church when it is faithful to Christ cannot cling to it. For the original message of the Church was about the future – about the coming of the kingdom of God, the beginning of God's complete rule. The first words spoken by Jesus in Mark's gospel (the first gospel written) are these: 'The time has come; the kingdom of God is upon you; repent and believe the Gospel.' That 'Gospel' or good news is about something bigger than the Church. The first Christians thought so highly of the Church to which they belonged that they pictured it as the bride of Christ – but with a passionate excitement they looked forward to something far better than the Church they knew. They looked forward to the total victory of Jesus. Almost the very last words of the Bible are these: '"Come!" say the Spirit and the bride. "Come!" let each hearer reply. Amen. Come, Lord Jesus!'

It may be that there is a glorious future ahead on this planet –

although it often looks as if we are going to mess things up completely. Scientists believe that the earth will be able to support human life for another two thousand million years to come. And it may be that Christians yet to be born will bring a glory into the Church's tradition far greater than any yet seen; it may turn out that up to AD 2000 Christianity was extremely primitive. Whatever the future is to be on this earth, long or short, glorious or tragic, Christians believe that it will lead to only one destination. At the end will come the final proof that, in his essential claims about God and God's creation, and in what he said about the supreme importance and power of love, Jesus Christ was right. So all human history – all the Church, but also everyone ever born – will be judged by one standard: how do you compare with Jesus Christ?

Writing to the Christians in Rome (chapter 8), Paul describes the Spirit given to Christians as 'the firstfruits of the harvest to come' – the bit of the crop that guarantees that the rest is on its way. In other words, the spiritual power which Christians do experience in their best moments is no more than a foretaste of what is promised. Paul writes of 'the splendour in store for us . . . the liberty and splendour of the children of God'. He says that we are going to be Christ-like, so that Jesus may be 'the eldest in a large family'. He asks triumphantly:

If God is on our side, who is against us? . . . How can he fail to lavish upon us all he has to give? . . . There is nothing in death or life . . . in the world as it is or in the world as it shall be, in the forces of the universe, in heights or depths – nothing in all creation that can separate us from the love of God in Christ Jesus our Lord.

According to the New Testament the Church's own life is meant to be a foretaste of the future. The letter to the Ephesians includes in its first chapter this prayer:

that you may know what is the hope to which God calls you, what the wealth and glory of the share he offers you among his people in their heritage, how vast the resources of his power open to us who trust in him . . . so that he might

display in the ages to come how great is his kindness to us in
Christ Jesus.

So a church building, set among people's homes, is meant to be
a reminder of the future which is now open to everyone. In
particular, every Holy Communion is a meal for travellers – and a
promise that God has prepared a banquet for all his children at
the end.

In different periods people tend to want different things from
the Church, because they hope for different things from the
future. For example, when Europe was full of barbarians who
killed and destroyed wherever they went, people longed for peace
– and the peace of a monastery was a foretaste, a pledge, a
guarantee of the peace of the world. When people's own homes
showed how poor they were, and how close they lived to disease
and death, they built and adorned churches. Many churches were
palaces for God and his people. Their beauty was a foretaste, a
pledge, a guarantee of the final 'City of God' – where no temple
would be needed. It is interesting to think out what are the most
powerful hopes of this generation. We still long for peace and
plenty; indeed, in our age of brilliant science and high tech-
nology, war and poverty on our rich planet seem to us more
outrageous than they have ever seemed in all history. But now
there is a special intensity of hope around the idea of unity.

We all know in our hearts that we desperately need a greater
sense of community, so that all the different groups that make up
modern society may work together for the common good,
overcoming their prejudices and settling their disputes on the
basis of fairness and justice. And we all know how completely the
nations of the modern world depend on each other, despite their
bitter suspicions and quarrels. We know that we need to share in
order to survive. For this reason, the twentieth century has asked
the Church: 'Do you have the secret of unity for a divided nation
and a divided world? Are you yourselves united? Do you
Christians love one another?'

Because the Church as we see it on this earth is people, not
angels – ordinary people, not saints – the Church is always
disappointing. The Church is so full of human imperfections that
we can easily pick holes in it, complaining about what it does and

about what it fails to do, condemning its failure. But we have to ask ourselves: if the fault lies with the people who make up the Church, are we ourselves any better? Are we in a position to criticize? Above all, are we entitled to stand aloof? Is it right for us to be proud that our hands are clean, when the reason is that we washed them too soon – or never did any work to get them dirty?

Each individual who is in touch with the Church is challenged for a few years to be the Church on this earth. The responsibility could not be greater, for according to the New Testament God has a purpose for everyone who is reached by the Church's message. It is not enough to criticize or applaud as spectators. The person who is challenged is expected to do something. God has a place for that one person – a place for him or her in the divine plan for the world, a place for him or her in the Church. That individual is invited to be a part of what is described in Peter's first letter (chapter 2): 'a royal priesthood, a dedicated nation, and a people claimed by God for his own, to proclaim the triumphs of him who has called you out of darkness into his marvellous light'.

If that person turns away, as Judas Iscariot did, he or she turns to the darkness, at least for the time being. That person's place may be given to someone else, or that piece of work for God's rule on earth and for the Church may be left undone for ever. But if that person accepts the calling of God through the voice of Jesus – if that person hears his or her name, as the first followers of Jesus heard their Master say 'Simon Peter!' or 'Mary!' – that person turns to the light and to the future.

The Church is changing fast. It may seem like winter but actually it is spring. The new music that is sung in many churches nowadays is only a small example of the renewal that is going on. Another example of change is that more and more responsibility is being taken by lay members of the Church – the 'royal priesthood' of Peter's letter. It is no longer possible to 'leave it to the vicar' ! In many ways lay members of the Church, particularly those who belong to the new generation, are using their imagination and courage. They are taking risks and making starts. Tact and perseverance are essential, for they have to persuade fellow-Christians who are conservative. But they are the people needed to rise to the future, to respond to the adventure of Jesus Christ.

Once when Jesus told a man to follow him, the man said that he would, one day – but he must stay at home until his father had died. Jesus replied that the future was more important. 'Follow me, and leave the dead to bury their dead.'

Of all the Christians who have lived so far, probably Paul had the best reasons for taking pride in how he had followed Jesus. But this is what he wrote to the Philippians (3:10–14), when he was near the end of his life, in prison in Rome. 'All I care for is to know Christ, to experience the power of his resurrection, and to share his sufferings . . . Forgetting what is behind me, and reaching out for what lies ahead, I press towards the goal to win the prize.' And that, surely, must be the spirit in which we are in the Church in our time. We get ready for the future, we reach out for what lies ahead – and, if need be, we forget the past.

But what should that mean in practice?

Making the future

Since the Church is people, not buildings – people, not doctrines – what is supremely important is the character of Christians. Whether we are loving matters far more than anything else. How we think and behave as people among other people (who watch!) is more important than how often we go to church. What the world needs and wants is a Church of living stones – a Church made up of people full of love. This is also what Jesus wants from his friends, as John's gospel makes clear in chapter 15. 'This is my commandment: love one another, as I have loved you. There is no greater love than this, that a man should lay down his life for his friends. You are my friends, if you do what I command you.'

Since most of our lives when not sleeping or eating is spent working, the most important contribution we can make to the welfare and progress of the world is to do useful work – and do it honestly and thoroughly.

This is the case whether our work is in our home, in a factory, in an office, in a shop, on a farm, or anywhere else. It is all serving other people, and so is serving the purposes of God. Very many Christians make their contribution through the professions which directly help others in their hours of need – as a priest, doctor, nurse, teacher or social worker. But thousands of other jobs are useful. Christian entertainers are needed, for example. So are Christian grocers, or miners, or politicians, or secretaries, or shop assistants, or business people, or waitresses, or pilots, or machine operators, or farmers, or computer experts, or refuse collectors . . . Christians, when they offer themselves to God, do not offer only Sundays or the evenings – they offer their work. They offer themselves as hard workers, honest, thorough and skilful. That does not mean, however, that they never criticize anything to do with their work. On the contrary, Christians work with their eyes open. They may ask awkward questions. Are the wages paid fair wages? Are the relationships between the people involved in the work as friendly as possible? Are the products being made, or services being given, as good as they can be, for the benefit of the people who need them?

Sometimes it is impossible to escape being unemployed for a period short or long, and surely God understands. And sometimes it is healthy and necessary to relax, with nothing to do – God knows that, too. But Jesus, as he bids farewell to his friends in John's gospel, speaks about what they will achieve by work, and it is right to extend the meaning of these words to cover all the work done faithfully by Christians. 'I am the vine, and you the branches. He who dwells in me, as I dwell in him, bears much fruit . . . This is my Father's glory, that you may bear fruit in plenty . . . I appointed you to go on and bear fruit, fruit that shall last.'

Since the world is a very practical place, Christians have to combine so that together they may set an example of love at work. A twentieth-century English saint, C. F. Andrews, who was a famous missionary in India, used to say: 'Love is the accurate estimate and supply of another's needs.' So Christians who work in the same place ought sometimes to get together, to ask themselves what their duty is in that place and how they can be better Christians at work. And Christians who live in the same district ought also to get together and ask themselves some practical questions. For a Christian congregation is meant to set an example to the neighbourhood in reaching and serving members of the community who need help.

When a congregation (or a group of congregations) organizes a playgroup for children, or when it runs a Sunday School, or when it supports an adventure playground or expeditions for children in the school holidays, or when it arranges groups of young people, or when it gathers a young wives' group or a women's fellowship or a branch of the Mothers' Union, or when it sponsors interesting activities for men, or when it gets visitors to keep in regular touch with old people and to help them if asked – then something practical and something Christian is being done, and the Church is serving others according to the example of its Lord, who washed his own disciples' feet.

Just the same thing is happening whenever Christians struggle for better housing in the neighbourhood, or for justice between the nations of the world, or when they collect money for charities such as Christian Aid (the British Churches' own charity to give relief to the victims of disasters and to help the poor peoples of the world to develop their own countries). Christians can wash the world's feet by serving in local government or in voluntary help to the local social services or the local hospital, or by being active in the local branch of a political party or trade union. It is all needed today – and it is all work for a better tomorrow.

The Christian Church was sent into the whole world – to every nation, tribe, city, town, shanty town or village without exception. It is sent to be compassionate wherever there is suffering and to be unyielding wherever there is injustice. Obviously it does not possess the resources in personnel or finance which governments have at their disposal, but the Church has immense spiritual resources. It has members within many situations of distress; it also has members who can bring valuable skills into those situations from outside; it can raise the funds which are needed to take action, usually on a small scale but in a way which erects a sign pointing to the kingdom of God.

That is why so many Anglicans have been among those who support the great charities which work for the rescue of people hit by a famine or other disaster, for the feeding, housing and resettlement of refugees, and for projects in development, offering assistance for self-help in escaping from the prison of long-term poverty. These agencies are able to work in close collaboration with local Christians, which gives some advantages over aid going through governments. The rise of charities such as Christian Aid, Oxfam and Tearfund was one of the true achievements of Christians in the twentieth century.

And that century was when Christians began to wake up to the fact that our planet is in great danger – not only from war and the modern weapons of war, but also from the thoughtlessness and greed which wage a 'peaceful' war against our own environment. We have polluted earth, air and water; we have destroyed or endangered many species among our fellow-creatures who cannot get away from us; we have used up many of the earth's resources in fuels, metals and minerals and our descendants may be bitter about that colossal consumption which has taken only a few years. The hope is that as a new century begins all these warnings are familiar – and, above all, the hope is that the comparatively few actions which have been taken to protect the environment will be increased.

Many Christians have already taken part in the necessary campaigns to alert public opinion and to repair the damage where possible. They have a special motive, as we saw in Chapter 2. The planet which we have so often treated so badly was not created by us or by our ancestors. It is the work of God. Therefore Christians honour the Creator when they respect the creation – and they serve God when they serve the cause of rescuing nature (as vulnerable as it is beautiful) from humanity's vandalism.

However, it is no less essential to carry on the work of telling the world about Jesus, what he has done and what he can do. Christians are not experts on 'how to be good', instructing completely ignorant sinners; we are much more like beggars telling other beggars how to get food. But the news we have heard is so good that we must pass it on, usually by how we live and work rather than by what we say. Obviously the chief challenge is to pass this message to those near to us – to people who are fellow-students, or in the office or factory or shop, or in our group of friends or our own families.

But we have an obligation to people who can be called foreigners, since every one of them is loved by the one Father. Christ died in order that we should have life, life as full as the Father wants it to be. Therefore since the eighteenth century Christian societies have been at work spreading the message brought by Christ; the best known of them are the Church Mission Society and the United Society for the Propagation of the Gospel, with the Society for Promoting Christian Knowledge which specializes in supplying Christian literature. These societies still need and deserve financial support – and above all their work needs Christians who are willing to live and work overseas in order to serve, strengthen and expand the Church there. Preachers and teachers are needed, but so are people with other skills.

By its missionary work the Christian Church has changed the world. In many countries the first modern schools and hospitals were started by Christians from overseas, and in all countries to which the Gospel has gone it has carried with it a new sense of the dignity, rights and responsibilities of every man, woman and child. This has been true even when people who believe themselves to be Christians have been among the oppressors and exploiters – for the Bible is dynamite which can explode even when the people in power try to ignore or hide what it teaches.

It is natural for a new generation to hope, and that is one of the reasons why the Church needs young people with their generosity, energy and daring. But Christian hope is not foolish optimism. That is why the Church also needs older people with their tested faithfulness. The world is a tough place, and in it anyone who wants to achieve anything worth achieving has to overcome many obstacles and has to possess patience. The courage of Christians is based not on expecting an easy life but on having a solid reason for going on being hopeful among the problems. In John's gospel (chapter 16), Jesus gives this reason when he tells his friends: 'You will be joyful, and no one shall rob you of your joy . . . I have told you all this so that in me you may find peace. In the world you will have trouble. But courage! The victory is mine; I have conquered the world.'

CHAPTER SIXTEEN

The heart of it all

The Silence of Eternity

You do look, my son, in a mov'd sort,
As if you were dismay'd: be cheerful, sir.
Our revels now are ended. These our actors,
As I foretold you, were all spirits and
Are melted into air, into thin air;
And, like the baseless fabric of this vision,
The cloud-capp'd towers, the gorgeous palaces,
The solemn temples, the great globe itself,
Yea, all which it inherit, shall dissolve
And, like this insubstantial pageant faded,
Leave not a rack behind. We are such stuff
As dreams are made on, and our little life
Is rounded with a sleep . . .

William Shakespeare (1564–1616)

Out of Silence a Voice

Love bade me welcome; yet my soul drew back,
    Guilty of dust and sin.
But quick-ey'd Love, observing me grow slack
    From my fit entrance in,
Drew nearer to me, sweetly questioning
    If I lack'd anything.

'A guest', I answered, 'worthy to be here':
    Love said, 'You shall be he.'
'I, the unkind, ungrateful? Ah, my dear,
    I cannot look on thee.'
Love took my hand, and smiling did reply,
    'Who made the eyes but I?'

'Truth, Lord, but I have marred them: let my shame
    Go where it doth deserve.'
'And know you not', says Love, 'Who bore the blame?'
    'My dear, then I will serve.'
'You must sit down', says Love, 'and taste my meat.'
    So I did sit and eat.

George Herbert (1593–1633)

Darkness

Wilt thou forgive that sin where I begun,
  Which was my sin, though it were done before?
  Wilt thou forgive that sin, through which I run,
  And do run still: though still I do deplore?
    When thou hast done, thou hast not done,
      For I have more.

Wilt thou forgive that sin which I have won
  Others to sin? and made my sin their door?
  Wilt thou forgive that sin which I did shun
  A year, or two: but wallowed in, a score?
    When thou hast done, thou hast not done,
      For I have more.

I have a sin of fear, that when I have spun
  My last thread, I shall perish on the shore;
  But swear by thyself, that at my death thy Son
  Shall shine as He shines now, and heretofore;
    And, having done that, thou hast done,
      I fear no more.

John Donne (1572–1631)

Light

Strong Son of God, immortal Love,
Whom we, that have not seen thy face,
By faith, and faith alone, embrace,
Believing where we cannot prove;

Thine are these orbs of light and shade;
Thou madest life in man and brute;
Thou madest Death; and lo, thy foot
Is on the skull that thou hast made.

Thou wilt not leave us in the dust:
Thou madest man, he knows not why;
He thinks he was not made to die;
And thou hast made him: thou art just.

Thou seemest human and divine,
The highest, holiest manhood thou;
Our wills are ours, we know not how;
Our wills are ours, to make them thine.

Our little systems have their day;
They have their day, and cease to be:
They are but broken lights of thee,
And thou, O Lord, art more than they.

We have but faith; we cannot know;
For knowledge is of things we see;
And yet we trust it comes from thee,
A beam in darkness: let it grow.

Let knowledge grow from more to more,
But more of reverence in us dwell;
That mind and soul, according well,
May make one music as before,

But vaster. We are fools and slight;
We mock thee when we do not fear:
But help thy foolish ones to bear,
Help thy vain worlds to bear thy light.

Alfred Tennyson (1809–92)

For discussion or for private thought

Chapter 1 introduces a little book about big questions. Which questions about religion are most important to you?

Chapter 2 outlines some reasons for believing that God is real. Which arguments seem to you strong, and which do you think are weak?

Chapter 3: When there is so much evil in the world, do you see why God should be called 'Father'?

Chapter 4: What do you think is the best way of understanding the stories of the death and resurrection of Jesus?

Chapter 5: Jesus is called 'Lord and Saviour'. What does this mean to you?

Chapter 6: Does 'the Holy Spirit' really mean 'our own bright ideas'?

Chapter 7: Should sexual activity be confined to marriage?

Chapter 8: 'Forgive and forget' – how are they different?

Chapter 9: Can a church which believes in freedom also be a strong church?

Chapter 10: What seems real to you in prayer?

Chapter 11: Should any babies be baptized?

Chapter 12: Is the Bible out of date?

Chapter 13: What are the strong points in the Anglican tradition – and what are the weak points?

Chapter 14: Does 'eat the flesh' and 'drink the blood' have to be essential in the twenty-first century?

Chapter 15: What ought to be changed in the Church? And who is to do it?

Index